LARGE EMPLOYERS AND APPRENTICESHIP TRAINING

Paul Ryan

Howard Gospel

Paul Lewis

Jim Foreman

The Chartered Institute of Personnel and Development is the leading publisher of books and reports for personnel and training professionals, students, and all those concerned with the effective management and development of people at work.
For full details of all our titles, please contact the Publishing Department:

Tel: 020 8612 6204

E-mail: publish@cipd.co.uk

To view and purchase all CIPD titles:
www.cipd.co.uk/bookstore

For details of CIPD research projects:
www.cipd.co.uk/research

LARGE EMPLOYERS AND APPRENTICESHIP TRAINING

Paul Ryan

Howard Gospel

Paul Lewis

Jim Foreman

KING'S COLLEGE, LONDON

First published 2006

Cover and text design by Sutchinda Rangsi-Thompson
Typeset by Paperweight
Printed in Great Britain by Antony Rowe

British Library Cataloguing in Publication Data
A catalogue record for this book is available from the British Library

ISBN   1 84398 167 X
ISBN-13   978 1 84398 167 1

Chartered Institute of Personnel and Development,
151 The Broadway, London SW19 1JQ

Tel: 020 8612 6200
Website: www.cipd.co.uk

Incorporated by Royal Charter. Registered charity no. 1079797.

CONTENTS

ACKNOWLEDGEMENTS

The CIPD would like to thank the research team and the organisations that assisted with this research. We would also like to thank Linda Clarke, Michelle Rogers, Lorna Unwin, John West and members of Sectors Skills Councils, employers' associations, the Department for Education and Skills, the Apprenticeships Task Force, and the Learning and Skills Council for their assistance.

LIST OF FIGURES AND TABLES

FOREWORD

Encouraging improvements in learning and development in the workplace is a core component of the CIPD's work. For many years apprenticeships have been a feature of workplace training in the UK, but with varying degrees of success. Within Government there is a renewed focus on promoting Advanced Apprenticeship and the public subsidies that aim to encourage employers to offer apprenticeships. However, take-up by large employers has been limited. Set this against a backdrop of frequently reported skills shortages and widespread criticism of the quality of the 'youth of today' entering the workforce, and it appears that although large-employer abstention from modern apprenticeship programmes is widely recognised, the reasons are not well understood.

In previous generations, large employers dominated industrial apprenticeship, and public subsidies were not available. The Government's Advanced Apprenticeship (AA) programme today offers grants of up to £15,000 for each apprentice who completes a training programme geared to intermediate skills (NVQ Levels 3–4). It is evident that increasing the number of apprentices is a high priority for Government. Yet few large employers appear on the list of Advanced Apprenticeship providers, and only a few 'missing' employers are involved in other ways – for example, through group training associations or as subcontracting providers of on-the-job training and work experience. Both features are comparatively recent developments.

Some large employers may still provide apprenticeship training along traditional lines, without any link to Advanced Apprenticeship and the associated subsidy. The continuing presence of apprenticeship activity, albeit at low levels, prior to the introduction of Advanced Apprenticeship, suggests that, while the practice had become less common than previously, it had not disappeared completely.

To help better understand what's going on in organisations, the CIPD commissioned a team at King's College London to undertake further research in this area. The focus of this work has been to gain a clearer overall understanding of large employer involvement in apprenticeship, including:

- ❖ establishing the nature and extent of large employers' involvement with Advanced Apprenticeship programmes, particularly as a source of intermediate skills

- ❖ examining the amount of 'apprenticeship' training that is provided by large employers without any link to Advanced Apprenticeship, and therefore government subsidy

- ❖ investigating the causes of involvement patterns amongst large employers

- ❖ considering possible ways of increasing the amount of intermediate-level skills learning sponsored by large employers

- ❖ asking whether the confidence that Government, and most recently the Modern Apprenticeship Advisory Committee, place in employer-sponsored apprenticeship is warranted, and how this may vary across sectors.

The research examines the nature of 'apprenticeship' in relation to the changing demographics of the workforce, and in particular the growing need to train 'adult' workers in intermediate skills. In England, the age limit on access to apprenticeships has technically been removed, but, with the exception of a small number of pilots, the effective age limit for eligibility for Advanced Apprenticeship funding largely remains at 25. This restriction reduces the involvement of some employers in Advanced Apprenticeship programmes. There is also a concentration of funding on those aged 19 and younger.

The research draws primarily on face-to-face interviews with learning and development managers in 30 large organisations. The organisations span the public and private sectors and include both UK- and internationally-owned examples. The research focuses on two sectors that have strong historical associations with apprenticeship programmes (engineering and construction) and two 'newer' sectors (retailing, and information and telecommunications technology).

The report explores the implications for organisational strategy and performance, as well as for national economic performance, so this research should be of interest to policy-makers and HR and learning and development professionals alike.

Victoria Winkler
CIPD Adviser, Learning, Training and Development
v.winkler@cipd.co.uk

EXECUTIVE SUMMARY

This research report considers the findings of a one-year research project concerning apprenticeships and large employers in Britain.

We define 'apprenticeship' generically, as an occupationally oriented training programme, aimed primarily or entirely at young people, that aims at intermediate (Level 3–4) skills and combines work-based learning with off-the-job training and technical education within a coherent learning package.

The research involved on-site interviews with learning and development-related managers in 30 large organisations in four sectors:

❖ engineering

❖ construction

❖ retailing

❖ information and communications technology.

The report considers two core linkages between large employers and apprenticeship:

❖ the contribution of apprenticeship in general, and the Advanced Apprenticeship programme in particular, to employers' supplies of intermediate skills

❖ the contribution of employers to the Advanced Apprenticeship programme.

The research examines the extent to which and reasons why 'apprenticeship' functions outside the Advanced Apprenticeship (AA) programme. The extent of non-AA apprenticeship proves quite limited. The primary reason for its existence is not a preference for bespoke programmes but rather the unavailability of public funding for particular categories of apprentice – notably adults, graduates and technicians.

The use that employers make of apprenticeship depends primarily on its cost-effectiveness relative to two alternative sources of skills – recruitment and upgrade training – within the employer's wider HR practices. Several large employers nowadays value apprenticeship as a source of long-term employment and career progression. At the same time, the government's efforts to expand apprenticeship are constrained by selective employer preferences for recruitment or upgrade training, or both.

The participation of large employers in Advanced Apprenticeship is examined in three dimensions.

❖ *Presence*. The involvement of employers is partial overall and highly variable across sectors and occupations. The most prominent influence appears to be the extent to which the employer values the technical learning content of Advanced Apprenticeship training frameworks – that is, the National Vocational Qualification and the Technical Certificate.

❖ *Scale and intensity*. Examining the number of apprentices relative to the overall number of employees in selected intermediate skills occupations shows that training intensity is highly variable. Ownership structures and community ties appear to make a considerable difference. Unlisted family firms with roots in local communities appear to train considerably more apprentices than do other employers.

❖ *Content*. The traditional approach to apprenticeship, in which the employer takes responsibility for all of the programme except its further education content, still dominates in engineering and telecommunications, but no longer in construction. Retailing employers tend to provide the entire programme in-house, but that may reflect the fact that the educational content of that sector's training programmes is more limited than in engineering and construction. There appears to be no simple relationship across sectors between the extent of employer responsibilities and training quality.

Further, we find that apprenticeship lives up only selectively to the government's aspiration that it become part of a ladder of vocational qualifications. Some employers actively support apprentice progression to tertiary studies, at Foundation or first degree level. Only rarely are more than a handful of individuals involved, however. Moreover, few employers support any extension of educational content for the average apprentice, even in the sectors in which the educational content of training programmes remains low.

Our research suggests that:

❖ in the right circumstances, employers do benefit from the introduction or expansion of apprenticeship training. This is particularly likely when skilled staff are difficult to recruit, when upgrade training cannot provide sufficient vocational knowledge, and when apprenticeship increases employee loyalty and reduces labour turnover.

❖ HR managers need to gather and assess information about the relative costs and benefits of the different types of training conducted within the organisation, notably apprenticeship and upgrading, and how both compare with recruitment.

❖ two particular potential benefits of apprenticeship deserve wider recognition, namely the scope for improving the selection and socialisation of young people who are prospective long-term employees, and the scope for promoting linkages between educational progression and career advancement within the organisation.

❖ the relatively high extent to which the content of Advanced Apprenticeship can be matched and tailored to the individual employer's requirements should be more widely appreciated, particularly in the 'new' training sectors.

❖ in some organisations the HR function appears to have only limited knowledge of its apprenticeship programmes, particularly when responsibility for that form of training falls to line management. In such cases, a greater integration of apprenticeship into the wider HR and training agenda appears desirable.

Some considerations for public policy also emerge.

❖ *Employer participation.* Employers' willingness to participate in Advanced Apprenticeship depends primarily on how they perceive the technical content of the recognised vocational qualifications. Were the content of these qualifications altered in the direction desired by employers, the willingness of employers to participate would increase. In retailing, that would, however, mean a reduction in the already limited content of the Technical Certificate.

❖ *Vocational education.* The Government's wish to see apprenticeship become part of a ladder of vocational qualifications has long been a reality in engineering and telecommunications. In construction and retailing, by contrast, its realisation would require the reform of training curricula – in particular, the injection of a more substantial component of technical education. Such changes cannot be expected from Sector Skills Councils at present, given the dominance of business interests in policy implementation and the Government's prioritisation of programme size over programme quality.

❖ *Appeal to young people.* Although the expansion of higher education has reduced the share of young people interested in apprenticeship, the programmes of most large employers still attract an excess supply of suitable applicants. Only in lower-paid sectors and occupations, including parts of retailing and construction, does the supply of potential apprentices to large employers' programmes warrant policy concern.

❖ *Apprenticeship activity.* It is desirable, given the needs both of individuals and the economy, for the apprenticeship programmes of some large companies to expand beyond the scale appropriate to their business requirements alone. How to engender that remains controversial, but one possibility is more cost-sharing for the more expensive skills. Some employers indicate a willingness to offer more apprenticeships, were more of the cost to be borne by other parties – a category that potentially includes apprentices themselves, public bodies and employer organisations.

❖ *Technician apprenticeship.* The limitation of LSC funding to Level 2–3 programmes has reduced the relative eligibility for public support of technician (Level 4) programmes. In sectors in which technician apprenticeship had already become established, including engineering, construction and telecommunications, the balance between its craft and technician components has been distorted. A rebalancing of public support between Level 3 and 4 programmes is desirable.

❖ *IT.* The scope for expanding apprenticeship is constrained with particular severity in IT (and in much of retailing) by employers' preference for graduate recruitment and upgrade training, and by high rates of labour mobility. It might be better to concentrate public effort on more promising terrain, and specifically to discourage Sector Skills Councils from diluting training standards in the quest for more apprenticeships.

❖ *Programme branding and coverage.* The Government has opted to apply the term 'Apprenticeship' to most DfES-funded programmes of work-based training for intermediate and lower level skills. That decision may have expanded training in some occupations. As, however, not all such training has been made eligible for public funding, some employers validly criticise the decision as having caused confusion over the meaning of 'apprenticeship'. The government might want to recognise the existence of non-AA apprenticeship, and to gauge its content, magnitude and causes more systematically than has been possible in this project.

Finally, we point to the variety of training practice and the amount of innovation on view in the case studies, much of it including apprenticeship. The confidence that the Modern Apprenticeship Advisory Committee placed in employer-sponsored apprenticeship appears broadly appropriate. The need, as always, is dual: first, to induce many of the large employers who currently provide high-quality apprenticeships to expand their programmes; and second, to raise programme quality in the sectors that are permitted, and even encouraged, to aim low, in educational terms.

INTRODUCTION 1

- ❖ **Intermediate skills remain important for employers, employees and the economy**

- ❖ **The report distinguishes between 'apprenticeships' and 'Apprenticeships' as sources of intermediate skills**

- ❖ **Four issues are central: apprenticeship as a source of intermediate skills; non-AA apprenticeship; the large employer and Apprenticeships, and the design and operation of Advanced Apprenticeship**

- ❖ **We focus on four sectors: engineering; construction; retailing, and information and communications technologies**

Contemporary Government policy towards apprenticeship reflects widely held concerns over skills, economy, and society. A limited skills base, particularly at the intermediate level to which apprenticeship traditionally contributed, is seen as having held back national economic performance; in terms of productivity and foreign trade (Prais, 1995; Oulton, 1996). A better apprenticeship system could be expected to contribute to the realisation of the Government's wish that British employers move up international league tables of value added and productivity.

> '...the traditional weakness of vocational education...impedes the raising of educational attainments to levels typical of other advanced economies.'

Secondly, the traditional weakness of vocational education, intensified by the decline of apprenticeship after the 1960s, impedes the raising of educational attainments to levels typical of other advanced economies (Gospel, 1994; Tomlinson, 2004). An expansion of apprenticeship would potentially counteract both problems. It could also be expected to improve youth employment prospects and school-to-work transitions more generally (Ryan, 2001).

This report investigates the relationship between large employers and apprenticeship, at a time of unprecedented Government promotion of both apprenticeship and full-time higher education. The two goals potentially conflict, insofar as the rapid expansion of participation in Higher Education reduces the supply of young people to apprenticeship.

This chapter outlines the context of our research, the issues investigated, and the methods used.

GOVERNMENT SUPPORT FOR APPRENTICESHIP

Contemporary Government support for apprenticeship dates back to the introduction, in 1994, of the Modern Apprenticeship programme, which evolved into what is nowadays called Advanced Apprenticeship (AA). Financial support has been geared to increasing apprentice numbers in traditional areas, notably engineering and construction, and to introducing apprenticeship into occupations from which it had previously been absent, including retailing and IT.

All training supported by Advanced Apprenticeship must contain a programme of learning that is recognised by the relevant Sector Skills Council (SSC) and contains three components:

- ❖ work-based learning geared to the acquisition of a National Vocational Qualification (NVQ) at Level 3

- ❖ off-the-job learning aimed at acquiring a Technical Certificate, also at Level 3

- ❖ learning geared to certification in at least two Key Skills – those related to numeracy and literacy – at Level 2.

The qualifications involved for each component must be accredited by the Qualifications and Curriculum Authority (QCA).

Programmes that meet these conditions are eligible for funding by the Learning and Skills Council (LSC) at rates that vary by training 'sector', age of entrant, and region. Current rates, for the occupational categories on which we focus, vary from around £4,500 for young adult entrants in IT and retailing, to nearly £15,000 for teenagers in engineering and telecommunications (see Appendix).

Figure 1 ❖ **Activity in government-funded work-based learning for young people, 1995–2004 ('000s in learning in Mar/Apr)**

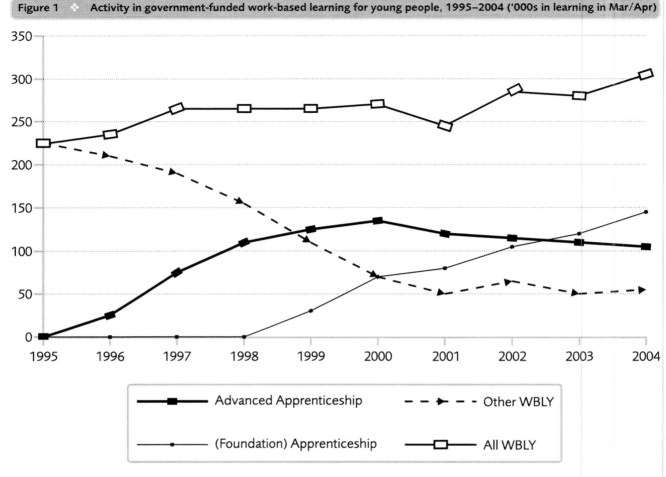

Source: DfES, *Statistical First Releases*: 03/2002, Table 2; 23.3.02, Table 2; SFR06, 22.3.05, Table 4

The focus of our study is work-based training programmes geared to intermediate skills. In traditional industrial parlance, these were 'craft' and 'technician' programmes; in contemporary terminology, they comprise work-based training aimed at Level 3 and 4 in the National Qualifications Framework.

> The focus of our study is work-based training programmes geared to intermediate skills.

All has not been well lately in publicly supported training for intermediate skills. Activity levels in Advanced Apprenticeship and its predecessors rose in the second half of the 1990s, but have since declined, both absolutely and as a share of publicly funded work-based learning for young people as a whole (see Figure 1).

By contrast, the number of Apprentices has continued to rise at lower skill levels. That trend provides some consolation for the decline at higher levels, particularly in terms of youth opportunities and social inclusion. The same cannot be said in terms of economic criteria. The decline in Level 3–4 apprenticeships, from levels already lower than those of apprenticeship-oriented economies on the continent (Ryan, 2000), is particularly threatening to the economic contribution of youth training.

'APPRENTICESHIP' VERSUS APPRENTICESHIP

This report distinguishes between 'apprenticeship' and 'Apprenticeship'. The former is a functional category; the latter, an administrative one. The criteria of programme content and public funding that lie behind the two categories are expected to overlap considerably in practice. But the two are conceptually and operationally distinct. Formal definitions of the two terms are provided in Box 1 opposite.

Our definition of apprenticeship accords with UK practice under the Training Boards of the 1970s, and with contemporary practice in continental Europe, Ireland, and Scotland (Ryan, 2001, 2004).

In implementing this approach, we take all of Advanced Apprenticeship to constitute apprenticeship, despite the limited educational content of some Technical Certificates. But we exclude from 'apprenticeship' the rest of the Apprenticeships programme (previously termed Foundation Apprenticeships), which is geared to skills below intermediate level.

We also include in 'apprenticeship' training programmes that do not come under the Advanced Apprenticeship scheme, whether or not they are termed apprenticeships by the employers that provide them, but that meet our functional criteria. Indeed, the scale of 'non-AA' apprenticeship is one of the project's leading issues. Examples include youth 'traineeships' in one telecommunications firm and adult (post-25) apprenticeships in three case studies in engineering and construction.

BOX 1 TERMINOLOGY: TWO CATEGORIES OF APPRENTICESHIP

'Apprenticeship' with an upper-case 'A' denotes nowadays work-based training programmes, aimed at both Level 2 and Level 3 vocational qualifications, that are recognised and supported by the Learning and Skills Council.

By 'apprenticeship' (with a lower-case 'a'), we mean occupational training programmes that aim at intermediate (Level 3–4) skills and qualifications and that combine work-based learning (including systematic task rotation) with off-the-job training and technical education, within a coherent learning package.

Finally, we exclude from 'apprenticeship' what may be termed upgrade training – that is, programmes that also aim at an intermediate skill level but that build on skills previously acquired by employees while working for their current employer. Upgrade training typically lacks either technical education or the integration of components that characterises apprenticeship proper. Examples include the technician training programme in one of the telecommunications case studies.

CORE ISSUES

In this report we study four core issues concerning apprenticeship and large employers:

❖ apprenticeship as a source of intermediate skills

❖ the scale of non-AA apprenticeship

❖ the large employer and Apprenticeships

❖ the design and operation of Advanced Apprenticeship.

Apprenticeship as a source of intermediate skills

Our first question is: to what extent, and why, do large employers use apprenticeship as a source of intermediate skills? Evidence on these issues can suggest ways to attain the goal of a larger apprenticeship system.

> From an employer standpoint, apprenticeship has drawbacks as well as advantages.

From an employer standpoint, apprenticeship has drawbacks as well as advantages. In particular, it has alternatives: first, the recruitment of individuals who are already skilled; second, the upgrade training of less skilled existing employees.

Either alternative may be more cost-effective than apprenticeship. Thus the limited size of the Advanced Apprenticeship programme may reflect the greater appeal of these alternatives to some employers. Similarly, the decline in Advanced Apprentice numbers in the decade to date, as shown previously in Figure 1, might reflect an increase in the appeal of one or both alternatives.

More generally, we enquire about the fit between apprenticeship and HR and training strategy. To what extent do large employers see apprenticeship training as suited to their approach to HR management? The potentially high cost of apprenticeship and the possibility that apprenticeship makes it easier for skilled employees to quit militate against choosing apprenticeship. To the extent, however, that training content can be tailored to the employer's specific requirements, or other advantages derived from it, such as the production of better skills, apprenticeship may be favoured by employers with a proactive HR policy.

The scale of non-AA apprenticeship

A second reason for the apparent weakness of any form of apprenticeship for intermediate skills, as judged by the number of Advanced Apprentices, might be that the latter is a poor guide to the former. Such would be the case, were employers to provide significant amounts of apprenticeship training outside the Apprenticeship programme.

Evidence that suggests significant numbers of non-programme apprentices includes the Labour Force Survey and reports by a large minority of learning and development managers that their employer offers apprenticeship-type training without government support (CIPD, 2005). Our second task within this report, therefore, is to seek direct evidence of apprenticeship training outside the Apprenticeships programme.

The large employer and Apprenticeships

> 'The organisations with whom the LSC contracts as 'prime sponsors'...include few employers in general...'

The next question is the involvement of large employers with the Advanced Apprenticeship programme. Concerns about this issue arose earlier this decade in response to some of the programme's operational attributes. The organisations with whom the LSC contracts as 'prime sponsors' to provide places on the Apprenticeships programme were found to include few employers in general, and few large, household name employers in particular. The apparently weak role of the large employer in Apprenticeships contrasted with its central one in traditional apprenticeship, which saw large factories, shipyards, and building sites with hundreds of apprentices apiece. The influential report of the Modern Apprenticeship Advisory Committee viewed the apparently marginal involvement of employers as a serious flaw in Modern Apprenticeship (MAAC, 2001).

The issue has since attracted both research and policy action. Analyses of provider lists have shown that the share of employers rises substantially when allowance is made for joint sponsorship through group training associations, Industrial Training Boards, employers' associations, and Chambers of Commerce (Gospel and Foreman, 2006). Some employers also participate only at arms length, almost invisibly, leaving the organisation of 'their' Apprenticeships to an external provider and confining their efforts to on-the-job training and work experience, and possibly an employment contract as well.

Adjustments for these omissions did not, however, change fundamentally the picture of limited involvement by large employers. The issue was seen officially as warranting policy activism on two fronts.

First, the LSC established the National Contracts Service specifically to involve more large employers in Apprenticeships, using direct marketing and funding and at company rather than district level. Progress has been made in bringing large employers on board, but the numbers involved remain limited.

Second, the Government set up the Apprenticeships Task Force, most of whose members were senior managers in large organisations. The first of the Task Force's 'key objectives' was 'to generate greater employer engagement in Apprenticeships' (Apprenticeships Task Force, 2005, Annex A). Its preferred modus operandi has been networking: the promotion of the programme to non-involved senior managers by those who are already involved (the 'champions'). The yield from its efforts appears to have been positive, but also limited (Apprenticeships Task Force, §29; Unwin and Fuller, 2004).

We distinguish here three aspects of employer participation in Advanced Apprenticeships: presence, extent, and content. Influential factors include the attributes of both the employer and the programme itself – or rather how managers perceive and evaluate the programme's attributes.

The design and operation of Advanced Apprenticeships

> A leading policy goal has been to make apprenticeship part of a 'vocational ladder' of educational attainment.

The fourth set of issues involves particular aspects of the design and operation of Advanced Apprenticeship. The first concerns its education-related functions, in terms of the age of apprentices, their completion rates and the extent to which the programme supports educational progression. The last of these is potentially important not only for young people and their parents, but also for

public policy (Steedman, Gospel and Ryan, 1998). A leading policy goal has been to make apprenticeship part of a 'vocational ladder' of educational attainment. The introduction into Apprenticeships of requirements for Key Skills and Technical Certificates reflected such educational aspirations.

We therefore consider the influence of Advanced Apprenticeship on large employers. One aspect is 'deadweight': how much 'bang' does the Government get for its 'buck', in terms of the effect on employers' training decisions? Many large employers operate customised HR practices. Are those practices altered by the inducements and requirements that come with the Apprenticeships programme, or do employers continue doing what they would otherwise have done without the programme?

Finally, we consider the prospective effects of the more employer-based specifications of training requirements – ie, the recognition for Advanced Apprenticeship purposes of employer-specific training programmes – that the Government is currently promoting in pursuit of increased participation by employers, particularly in retailing and IT. To what extent do these changes weaken the educational functions that government wishes Apprenticeships to perform?

SCOPE AND METHODOLOGY

We focus our attention on four sectors: engineering, construction, retailing and information and communications technologies (ICT), which account for around half of activity in Advanced Apprenticeship (Table 1, opposite).

The gap between training activity in the 'traditional' (engineering, construction) frameworks and the 'modern' ones (retailing and ICT) is increasing (Table 2, opposite), and the completion rates in engineering and ICT are roughly double those in retailing (Table 3, opposite).

For the purposes of this research, intermediate vocational skills are taken to be primarily – but neither exclusively nor exhaustively – those located at Levels 3 and 4 of the National Qualifications Framework. A 'large employer' is one with at least 1,000 employees. However, the decentralisation of decision-making in many large organisations means that many of the business units that we study number their employees only in the hundreds – and in the occupational categories on which we focus, sometimes only in the dozens.

We undertook between six and nine case studies in each of the four sectors. The organisations include non-profit and public bodies. Our principal research method was face-to-face interviews with senior learning and development managers in 30 case-study organisations. Table 4, on pp 6–7, lists their ownership and employment attributes. The four organisations – two Japanese-owned engineering companies, one IT company, and a Borough Council – that insisted on confidentiality are given pseudonyms.

The intermediate skills chosen for investigation are indicated by the occupational categories in Table 5 on pp 8–9. Employment in those categories amounts in most cases to only a small proportion

Table 1 ❖ Advanced Apprenticeship: number of leavers by area of learning, 2002–03 ('000)

Area of learning	Number	%
Engineering, technology, manufacturing	15,100	24.8
Construction	5,700	9.4
Information and communication technology	1,800	3.0
Retailing, customer service, transportation	8,500	13.9
All four areas	31,100	51.2
All areas of learning	60,800	100.0

Source: DfES, Statistical First Release SFR04, 29.6.04, Table 8
Note: includes non-completers

Table 2 ❖ Number of participants on LSC-funded work-based learning by area of learning, 2002–04

	Numbers ('000) 2002	2002	Indices 2003	2004
Engineering, technology, manufacturing	67.0	100.0	108.3	111.9
Construction	33.1	100.0	110.6	116.0
Information and communication technology	9.5	100.0	78.9	62.1
Retailing, customer service, transportation	36.1	100.0	103.0	95.8
All four areas	145.7	100.0	105.6	105.6
All areas of learning	286.7	100.0	110.0	113.5

Source: DfES, Statistical First Releases, ILR/SFR06, 22.3.05, Table 2; ILR/SFR03, 31.3.04, Table 2
Notes: Data are for 'numbers in learning', including other (non-AA) programmes, on 1 October (1 November for 2002)

Table 3 ❖ Completion of entire framework[a] by area of learning, Advanced Apprenticeship, 2001–03 (% leavers)

Area of learning	2001–02	2002–03
Engineering, technology, manufacturing	35	46
Construction	38	31
Information and communication technology	31	41
Retailing, customer service, transportation	16	20
All[b]	26	32

Source: DfES, Statistical First Release SFR04, 29.6.04, Table 8
Notes: a. NVQ3, Technical Certificate and Key Skills
          b. All frameworks recognised under Advanced Apprenticeship

Table 4 ❖ **Attributes of case-study organisations: ownership and employment**

Sector	Case study	Location	Ownership		No. of employees
			Parent	Status	
Engineering	J.C. Bamford Excavators Ltd	Rocester, Staffs	–	For profit, unquoted (family)	4,500
	Marshall Aerospace Ltd	Cambridge	Marshall Group	For profit, unquoted (family)	1,500
	Perkins Engines Company Ltd	Peterborough	Caterpillar Inc.	For profit, quoted	3,500
	Rolls-Royce plc	Derby	Rolls-Royce International	For profit, quoted	21,000
	Siemens Standard Drives	Congleton	Siemens AG	For profit, quoted	350
	PARTSCO	(Britain)	(Japanese company)	For profit, quoted	6,000
	STEAMCO	(Scotland)	(Japanese company)	For profit, quoted	10,500
Construction	Carillion Construction Training	London	Carillion plc	For profit, quoted	20,000[a]
	Laing O'Rourke Learning World	Dartford Nottingham	Laing O'Rourke Learning World	For profit, quoted	10,000[a]
	Leicester City Council Maintenance DSO	Leicester	Leicester City Council	Public sector	650
	McNicholas plc	London	McNicholas plc	For profit, quoted	1,500
	Morrison Construction	Sutton Coldfield	Anglian Water Group	For profit, quoted	7,000
	Mowlem Building, South West	Bath	Mowlem Group	For profit, quoted	250
	NG Bailey & Company Ltd	Ilkley	NG Bailey Organisation Ltd	For profit, unquoted (family)	3,500
Retailing	Bells Stores	Skelton	J. Sainsbury plc	For profit, quoted	1,000
	Ipswich and Norwich Co-operative Society	Ipswich	Self	For profit, unquoted (co-op)	3,500
	John Lewis	London	The John Lewis Partnership	For profit, unquoted (co-op)[c]	63,000
	Lincolnshire Co-operative Ltd	Lincoln	Self	For profit, unquoted (co-op)	2,700
	Pilot Outlet Limited	Swansea	Chesterfield Properties Limited	For profit, unquoted	n.a.
	Selfridges & Co	London	Wittington Investments Ltd	For profit, unquoted	4,000
	Tates Limited	Willenhall	A.F. Blakemore & Son Ltd	For profit, unquoted	3,600

Table 4 ❖ **Attributes of case-study organisations: ownership and employment (cont)**

Sector	Case study	Location	Ownership		No. of employees
			Parent	Status	
Retailing (cont)	Tesco plc	Welwyn Garden City	Self	For profit, quoted	237,000
	The Co-operative Group	Glasgow	Self	For profit, unquoted (co-op)	40,000
ICT	BT Retail	Sunderland	BT plc	For profit, quoted	36,000
	BT Global Services	Swindon	BT plc	For profit, quoted	6,000[b]
	DATACO	(Britain)	(Wholly owned subsidiary)	For profit, quoted	4,000
	Data Connection Ltd	Enfield	Employee trust	For profit, unquoted (co-op)[c]	300
	BIGBORO	(England)	Self	Public sector: local authority	15,000
	LogicaCMG Outsourcing	London	Self	For profit, quoted	21,000
	Siemens Traffic Controls	Poole	Siemens AG	For profit, quoted	700

Notes: Parentheses indicate information concealed to protect anonymity

a. Parent organisation
b. UK operations only
c. Owned by an employee trust

of total employment, and to fewer than a hundred in five cases, all in engineering or ICT. The number of entering apprentices is even smaller: in most cases fewer than fifty, and in many fewer than twenty, a year.

The following six chapters consider the four core issues as follows: the sources of intermediate skills (Chapter 2); the scale and nature of 'non-AA' apprenticeship (Chapter 3); the pattern and determinants of employer participation in Advanced Apprenticeship in terms of presence, scale and intensity, and content (Chapters 4 to 6); and the programme's design and operation (Chapter 7). The conclusions follow in Chapter 8. The appendix discusses further the context, scope, and method of the research.

Table 5 ❖ **Attributes of case-study organisations: intermediate skills and apprenticeship training**

Sector	Case study	Intermediate skills Occupations covered	Intermediate skills Employment	Advanced Apprenticeship Participate	Advanced Apprenticeship Contract holder	Apprenticeship intake[a]
Engineering	J.C. Bamford Excavators Ltd	Toolroom and maintenance design and craft	90	yes	External provider (Burton College)	8
	Marshall Aerospace Ltd	Engineering craft and technician	750	yes	Self	38
	Perkins Engines Company Ltd	Engineering craft and technician	425	yes	Self	18
	Rolls-Royce plc	Fitters, engine testers, technicians, maintenance	9,500	yes	Self	66
	Siemens Standard Drives	Electronics, IT and engineering technicians	40	no	–	0
	PARTSCO	Maintenance craft, production engineers	30	no	–	0
	STEAMCO	Engineering and construction, craft and technician	2,500	yes	External provider (ECITB)	60
Construction	Carillion Construction Training	Construction trades	n.a.	yes	Self (training subsidiary)	250[d]
	Laing O'Rourke Learning World	Construction trades	7,000	yes	Self (joint venture)	20[d]
	Leicester City Council Maintenance DSO	Construction, electrical and plumbing trades	500	yes	External providers (JTL, Leicester College)	14
	McNicholas plc	Construction trades, especially road work	700	no	–	0
	Morrison Construction	Construction trades	300	yes	External provider (CITB)	15
	Mowlem Building, South West	Construction trades	145	yes	External provider (CITB)	8
	NG Bailey & Company Ltd	Electrical, heating and ventilating, plumbing	1,050	yes	Self	60
Retailing	Bells Stores	Store manager, assistant store manager	200	yes	Self	15
	Ipswich and Norwich Co-operative Society	Store manager, deputy store manager	130	yes	Self	22
	John Lewis	Section manager, department manager	5,500	no	–	0

Table 5 ❖ **Attributes of case-study organisations: intermediate skills and apprenticeship training (cont)**

Sector	Case study	Intermediate skills Occupations covered	Employment	Advanced Apprenticeship Participate	Contract holder	Apprenticeship intake[a]
Retailing (cont)	Lincolnshire Co-operative Ltd	Store manager, supervisor	850	yes[b]	External provider (LAGAT)[c]	0
	Pilot Outlet Limited	Store manager, deputy store manager	n.a.	yes	Self	n.a.
	Selfridges & Co	Team leader, merchandiser, specialist, manager	500	no	–	0
	Tates Limited	Store, area and regional manager; department head	300	no	–	0
	Tesco plc	Section manager, team leader	n.a.	no	–	0
	The Co-operative Group	Junior manager	3,000	yes	External provider (Manchester Enterprises)	28
ICT	BT Retail	T/C field service engineer, technician	18,000	yes	External provider (Accenture)	400
	BT Global Services	T/C field service engineer, technician	5,000	yes	External provider (Accenture)	42
	DATACO	IT software programmer	350	no	–	0
	Data Connection Ltd	IT equipment and systems operator	20	no	–	0
	BIGBORO	Computer operator, IT technician	20	no	–	0
	LogicaCMG Outsourcing	IT operation and support staff	250	no	–	0
	Siemens Traffic Controls	T/C field service engineer, technician	340	no	–	8

Notes: n.a.: not available
a. Apprentices starting programme in current year or most recent year for which data are available
b. Currently withdrawing from Advanced Apprenticeship in retailing
c. Contract formerly held by the employer
d. Participants in Level 2 programme who continue to Level 3

SECURING THE SUPPLY OF INTERMEDIATE SKILLS

2

❖ **Apprenticeship is seen by some employers as providing better, and more loyal, employees than recruitment**

❖ **The contrast between upgrade training and apprenticeship is sometimes weaker than supposed**

❖ **Apprenticeship is often found to align well with broad HR strategy**

INTRODUCTION

This chapter considers the advantages and drawbacks of apprenticeship as a source of intermediate skills for large employers. Much of the policy literature on the issue is impaired by an advocacy stance, which typically outlines the merits of apprenticeship in detail but neglects its limitations.

Two alternative sources of intermediate skills must be considered: recruitment and upgrade training. Recruitment provides new employees who are already skilled; upgrade training builds the skills of existing employees up to intermediate level. Apprenticeship often competes against both. This chapter considers the employer's choice between the three alternatives. What is in principle a three-way choice is decomposed for simplicity into a pair of two-way ones: that between recruitment and training, and, to the extent that training is chosen, that between upgrade training and apprenticeship.

The two choices are treated not as 'either or' ones, but rather as matters of emphasis and degree – for example, where to pitch the balance between training and recruitment.

We consider the choice between these alternatives from the perspectives of both labour economics and HR strategy. The labour economics approach emphasises the relative cost of the alternatives as a source of skilled employees, with particular attention to their effects on turnover among skilled employees. The HR approach emphasises the alignment of the various alternatives with the employer's wider HR practices, with particular attention to their implications for employee motivation, loyalty, and productivity.

THE SOURCES OF INTERMEDIATE SKILLS

Before these issues are investigated, we describe the practices that case-study employers adopt in securing their supplies of intermediate skills. The variety of employer practice can be illustrated by three cases, each of which relies primarily on one of the alternatives: NG Bailey on apprenticeship, Siemens Standard Drives on upgrade training, and DATACO on recruitment.

> ## BOX 2 DIFFERING SOURCES OF INTERMEDIATE SKILL: BAILEY, SIEMENS STANDARD DRIVES, DATACO
>
> These three employers respectively prefer apprenticeship, upgrade training and recruitment as the principal source of intermediate skills.
>
> Bailey (more widely known as NG Bailey) is the principal subsidiary of a long-established, family-owned supplier of building services to large construction projects. Around half of its craft electricians and many of its technical and management staff – exceptionally high shares for the construction industry – are products of the company's own apprenticeship programmes. The apprentice headcount is nowadays nearly one-third as large as skilled manual employment. The prominence of apprenticeship reflects its contribution to competitive advantage, as a key contributor to the company's reputation for work of high quality.
>
> Siemens Standard Drives manufactures electronic speed controllers for electric motors. Most of its 40 technician employees acquired their skills internally, by upgrade training as production workers. The upgrading involves a three-year Ordinary National Certificate (ONC) course

in electronics, taught at the works by the staff of a local college. All of the latest group of upgrade trainees completed the ONC; nearly half subsequently took a more advanced course. The required skills can rarely be recruited directly. Apprenticeship has in the past been used for IT skills, but upgrading is preferred for technicians on grounds of cost, labour turnover, and adaptation to manpower requirements (as it is made available only in anticipation of future vacancies).

DATACO processes and analyses confidential data for financial institutions. Its 'Implementation Section' has around 170 employees at intermediate level, principally software programmers for mainframe applications. The great majority of its skilled employees were recruited externally, mostly in their thirties. High pay and low labour turnover have made it possible to rely heavily on recruitment, except during a rapid expansion some years ago, when less skilled non-graduates were recruited into a temporary six-week course of uncertified upgrade training. Apprenticeship has not featured, as Advanced Apprenticeship is seen as unsuitable for the employer's requirements, in terms of its mandated qualifications and administrative burden.

The three cases in Box 2 are chosen to illustrate the range of employer practice, and not to suggest that the three sources of intermediate skills are mutually exclusive. Indeed, none of the three employers relies only on one source. For example, recruitment and apprenticeship each account for roughly half of NG Bailey's employment of intermediate skills.

More generally, various combinations of the three approaches are visible. One method combines recruitment and upgrade training. Two variants of this may be distinguished.

The first is to recruit people who have acquired partial occupational skills and then fill in the gaps by upgrade training. This method is widespread in construction, which nowadays sees many partially and informally trained workers in such trades as bricklaying, plastering, and decorating receive upgrade training, aimed at a Level 2 NVQ. The practice is encouraged by the Construction Skills Certification Scheme, which aims at having all manual employment on building sites qualified to at least NVQ Level 2. A prominent example of the practice is provided by the building contractor Laing O'Rourke.

The second variant is to recruit graduates and give them further training to meet the employer's requirements. This method is common in IT, which sees many employers train recently recruited graduates in particular programming and systems skills. An example is provided by Data Connection.

More generally, and perhaps not surprisingly, most case-study employers make more use of recruitment or upgrade training, or both, than of apprenticeship. The employer's own apprenticeships account for half or more of skilled employment in only five of our case studies, including, in addition to Bells Stores in retailing and NG Bailey in construction, three engineering employers – Marshall Aerospace, J.C. Bamford, and Perkins Engines.

RECRUITMENT AND TRAINING

To what extent, and why, do employers opt to recruit already skilled labour rather than train up the relevant skills themselves?

> 'The economics of skills...concludes that the threat of poaching discourages training and encourages recruitment.'

The choice between recruitment and training evokes the long-standing controversy over the 'poaching' of skilled labour – ie the incentive to employers to free-ride on the training efforts of other employers by recruiting employees they have trained. The economics of skills that are both costly to produce and transferable between employers – as are many intermediate skills – concludes that the threat of poaching discourages training and encourages recruitment. Any employer who offers training for such skills provides an 'externality' – a benefit to other employers for which it is not itself compensated. The labour market consequently fails to deliver enough training.

Market failure is not, however, absolute. Recruitment becomes more expensive when employers as a whole do less training, as skilled workers become correspondingly hard to find and retain. Employers are therefore expected to use both recruitment and training, but not to provide enough of the latter – that is, collectively to produce fewer skilled workers than they would like to employ (Stevens, 1995).

The poaching externality provided the rationale for the levy-grant arrangements operated by the Industrial Training Boards (ITBs) in the 1970s. Employers who rely on recruitment were required to compensate those who provide training, thereby reducing the externality and curbing market failure. The two ITBs that still function are both in construction, where high rates of labour turnover, associated with site-based employment, create particularly strong disincentives to training.

From an HR perspective, training is viewed as part of the employer's wider employment practices, which are chosen so as to maximise the motivation, loyalty, and productivity of employees. The CIPD report *Understanding the People and Performance Link: Unlocking the black box* (Purcell *et al*, 2003) highlighted the importance of training and development. It found that 'effective firms have a level of sophistication in their approach to people management which helps induce discretionary behaviour and above-average performance'. As the 'fit' between training, job content, and other HR practices becomes tighter, so the benefits of training can be expected to accrue more to the employer who provides it than to its competitors (MacDuffie, 1995).

The evidence also suggests that the adoption of particular sets of HR practices contributes to productivity and profitability (Guest et al., 2003). Moreover, by socialising employees into the employer's way of operating and forming part of a career employment perspective, employer-based training may reduce, not increase, turnover among skilled employees (Green, 2000).

The contrast between the view of training associated with labour economics and HR strategy is far from absolute. The HR approach does not rule out concern on the part of employers over the prospective loss of investments in training as a result of labour turnover. It simply suggests that, if training reduces the propensity of employees to quit, the disincentive to train is weaker than standard economic models take it to be. The employer would then be expected to use training – including apprenticeship – more and recruitment less than economic models predict.

The case studies suggest various factors that affect the appeal of recruitment relative to training.

The first is the relative cost of the alternatives. The cost of recruitment is low when the supply of labour in the external market is plentiful and there is little competition for it from other employers. In such cases, recruitment is normally the preferred option. Thus establishments located where unemployment is high, as in industrial areas in the north of England, tend to use recruitment more than those located in the south east, where it is low.

For example, in ICT, the location of DATACO's Implementation Section and Logica CMG's Outsourcing Division in declining industrial areas allows both companies to rely heavily on recruitment. In engineering, PARTSCO, a Japanese-owned company with a manifest commitment to employee development, relies almost entirely on recruitment for its skilled labour. It benefits from continuing lay-offs of craft engineers by other employers in a locality with persistently high unemployment. Similarly, in construction, an already extensive use of recruitment has expanded recently as a result of the ready availability of skilled immigrant labour, from Eastern Europe in particular.

At higher occupational levels, where graduates are involved and labour markets are regional or national, the cost of recruitment may remain moderate even though local unemployment is low – as in the case of Data Connection, located in a London suburb.

'...recruitment is used more extensively when labour requirements are less stable.'

Secondly, recruitment is used more extensively when labour requirements are less stable. The extreme case is construction, where labour needs are project- and site-based, and therefore temporary and moveable. Many skilled workers do not wish to move around the country alongside any particular employer's building contracts. Similar conditions are present for specialist IT employers, whose teams of specialists assemble to execute specific projects in specific locations.

The result is the use of fixed-term contracts, along with high lay-off rates and reliance on recruitment when new projects begin or product demand rises. The majority of the skilled workforce of four construction-related cases (Laing O'Rourke, Morrison, Leicester Council DSO, and STEAMCO) and four ITC ones (DATACO, Data Connection, Logica CMG, and Siemens Traffic Controls) were obtained by recruitment, usually combined with upgrade training.

Even when labour needs are attached indefinitely to one location, as in most of manufacturing, if product demand fluctuates, so too do the employer's labour requirements, thereby creating a role for

recruitment. Thus, in engineering, Marshall Aerospace, Perkins Engines and Rolls-Royce (Derby) use recruitment specifically to handle cyclical fluctuations in labour requirements, on top of training for their trend requirements. High cyclicality in product demand means that a large minority of craft employees has been recruited externally, notwithstanding the importance all three companies attach to training and development.

A further advantage of recruitment is the potential benefit of using an already experienced employee rather than a trainee. Two aspects are emphasised. The first is a variation on low relative cost. Some employers find the immediate productivity of a skilled recruit much greater than that of a trainee – in terms of 'hitting the ground running', according to a manager at Mowlem. Secondly, recruits may be valued, as notably in retailing by Tesco, John Lewis, Selfridges, and Pilot Outlet, for the fresh ideas and awareness of external best practice that many bring with them.

Under such circumstances, recruitment is the preferred source of skills, used as extensively as possible without driving its cost too high. In that sense, the 'business case', which is often said in policy discussions nowadays to favour training in general and apprenticeship in particular, often points in the first instance to recruitment instead.

'Recruitment sometimes costs more than training.'

Nevertheless, recruitment does not dominate training in our cases taken as a whole. The factors that favour recruitment in some circumstances discourage it in others. The first factor is relative cost. Recruitment sometimes costs more than training. In sectors characterised by low pay and high labour turnover, recruitment tends to be expensive and the scope for using it limited. Thus, in convenience store retailing, Bells Stores and the two regional retail co-operatives face a scarcity, in both quantity and quality, of management skills in the external labour market. All would willingly recruit more managers were it easier to do so.

The cost of recruitment can also be high in well-paid employment, as in aerospace and engineering construction. Marshall Aerospace finds that specialist recruitment agencies charge high fees, and many recruits need expensive upgrade training. STEAMCO reports that the qualifications of foreign skilled workers are often not recognised internationally as valid for use in power station projects around the world, which also means expensive upgrade training.

Secondly, the use of recruitment is also discouraged when labour requirements are stable, for high-wage employers at least. Thus, while Perkins Engines uses recruitment to meet fluctuations in its skill requirements, steady demand for its products in recent years means that only a small minority of its craft employees have been recruited externally.

A third consideration is that, although recruits are often experienced and well informed, their other traits may be less attractive. Many employers express reservations about the quality of the average recruit. The defects mentioned are: overall quality as employees, in terms either of a low average or a high variability; lack of important skills; unsuitable attitudes; difficulty of being inculcated with the company's culture, which means higher training costs; and a quit rate higher than that of ex-trainees.

> 'Many employers express reservations about the quality of the average recruit.'

The importance of these limitations is indicated by the limited role that recruitment plays in some organisations whose circumstances, in both product and labour markets, might be expected to favour it. In construction, both Mowlem (South West) and NG Bailey state that although they cannot avoid using recruitment, they prefer training where possible and obtain only a minority of their skilled employees – 20% and 48% respectively – directly from the outside.

The upshot is a widespread reluctance to rely on recruitment, as opposed to just giving it a significant role, as a source of intermediate skills.

UPGRADE TRAINING AND APPRENTICESHIP

When an employer chooses to provide training, is upgrade training or apprenticeship favoured?

Upgrade training is a diverse category. For production workers, it traditionally involved informal and uncertified forms of learning on the job, including simple 'learning by doing'. Similar attributes applied at a higher level of skill in the case of managers. Nowadays upgrade training remains mostly job-based and uncertified, but it more often involves formalised, structured learning. It also tends to involve adults rather than young employees.

In the context of intermediate skills, we characterise upgrade training in terms of programmes: that prepare employees for more skilled jobs as they move up a job or promotion ladder; that may be given to recent recruits but focus primarily on established employees; and that are often given to employees who have spent longer in full-time education than have apprentices, as notably for IT-related occupations.

Labour economics and HR strategy have much in common when it comes to explaining the choice between upgrade training and apprenticeship. In standard accounts, apprenticeship, with its orientation to certified, transferable skills, is expected to rate lower with employers than upgrade training, with its orientation to uncertified skills specific to the particular employer's requirements.

Economic models of internal labour markets (ie, career employment structures within particular organisations), including Japanese-type employment practices, see upgrade training as favoured when skills are specific to the employer, whether as a result of technological necessity or employer choice. The employer seeks to reduce the amount invested and the risk of not making a return on that investment because of quits. One response is to opt for the upgrade training of established employees. The content of that training can be tailored to the employer's requirements. The training can be delivered

sequentially, in discrete doses linked to employee induction and career progression, thereby limiting the size and riskiness of the investment in skills (Wachter and Wright, 1990).

> '...apprenticeship...involves the employer in an investment in each trainee that is larger, more front-loaded, and more vulnerable to quits.'

The contrast with apprenticeship is potentially sharp. First, apprenticeship concentrates a large amount of vocational learning into a single, up-front, multi-year programme – attributes that make it potentially expensive, particularly in the absence of public subsidies. Second, the skills learned are highly transferable to other employers, geared as the training is to external occupational standards rather than the needs of the employer providing the training – attributes that make it easier for skilled workers to quit. Third, apprenticeship tends to be taken by young workers, often straight out of full-time education and not yet established in a lasting match with the employer who is training them, and therefore with a high, age-related, propensity to quit. Relative to upgrade training, apprenticeship therefore involves the employer in an investment in each trainee that is larger, more front-loaded, and more vulnerable to quits (Marsden and Ryan, 1991; Ryan, 1994).

Similarly, an HR-oriented analysis might suggest that employers would favour upgrade training over apprenticeship when it comes to maximising employee motivation and loyalty. Training can focus on the values and priorities of the organisation when it is given informally to existing employees and no external certification is involved. The prospect of sequential doses of upgrade training, delivered as needed during progress along an employer's promotion ladders, contributes to employee motivation and loyalty.

At the same time, upgrade training and apprenticeship may act as complements rather than alternatives in the development of intermediate skills. The traditional concept of apprenticeship, a source of skill and knowledge sufficient for a full working life, has been undermined by rapid change in technologies and product markets. Craft, technician, and professional workers alike must nowadays upgrade their skills during their working lives if they are to remain employable. Conversely, employers who seek to motivate and tie in employees by providing opportunities for continuing training may benefit from the prior vocational education that apprenticeship at its best provides. Such prior learning may be necessary if adult employees are to make good use of upgrading opportunities.

The comparative advantages of upgrade training and apprenticeship, as seen by our case-study employers, align in some respects with those emphasised by both the economics and the HR perspectives, but in others diverge in favour of apprenticeship. Differences across employers and sectors prove substantial.

One background factor must be recognised at the outset: the level that skill requirements are pitched at. Upgrade training tends to appeal to employers for jobs whose skill requirements lie either below intermediate level, such as those of most production and office employees, or above them, such as those of managers. Apprenticeship – in the generic sense – tends to appeal more to employers for jobs that require intermediate skills, such as those of craft, technician, and assistant professional workers. Upgrade training might be expected therefore to dominate the more routine production and office jobs; apprenticeship, less routine ones in production, maintenance and design.

The sectors covered here differ considerably in this respect. Although all in principle involve intermediate skills, their skill requirements differ considerably. Within Level 3 programmes, skill requirements are markedly lower, in terms of training times, training costs and pubic subsidies alike, in retailing than in engineering and telecommunications. Moreover, the blurring of the boundary between Levels 2 and 3 in construction brings into the scope of this report many Level 2 'trades' in that sector. The greater appeal of upgrade training in retailing and construction than in engineering and telecommunications reflects to some extent lower skill levels in the former than in the latter sectors.

> 'Where upgrade training aims at the same skill level as does apprenticeship, it often proves superior in terms of cost, speed, and flexibility.'

Holding skill level constant, other determinants of employer preference between upgrade training and apprenticeship are apparent. Where upgrade training aims at the same skill level as does apprenticeship, it often proves superior in terms of cost, speed, and flexibility. Concerning costs, Siemens Standard Drives has reduced the cost of technician training by moving from apprenticeship to upgrade training (as shown in Box 1). Several attributes reduce its training costs, compared with those of apprenticeship. Training content is limited to class-work for the Technical Certificate. Trainees perform normal production work when not doing class-work. Instruction occurs at the workplace, not at a college on day release. As the two hours of classwork a week are timed to fall evenly on each side of the time at which the late shift replaces the early shift, for each trainee only one of the two hours is paid time – by contrast to conventional day release, in which class time is paid in full.

These cost-related advantages for upgrade training are particularly important for producers of intermediate goods, whom large clients press continuously to lower their product prices. But they apply more widely, and are cited by BT, McNicholas, and Selfridges among others.

Some employers – including McNicholas and Tates, as well as Siemens Standard Drives – favour upgrade training for the ease of adjusting its content and availability to changing skills requirements. The praise that Mowlem and Lincolnshire Co-op bestow on upgrade training for its 'flexibility' presumably denotes similar attributes.

The reported advantages of upgrading also include the screening of potential skilled employees. Siemens Standard Drives sees screening as more effective when conducted on-the-job, as is normal in upgrading, than before employment, as normally in apprenticeship. Similarly, the recent decision by J.C. Bamford to introduce an upgrade programme for engineering skills alongside its apprenticeships reflects an increased interest in on-the-job screening, using its knowledge of the qualities of established employees, in addition to a scarcity of suitable young applicants for apprenticeship.

Some employers also report positive effects on employee motivation and loyalty from upgrade training for intermediate skills. Examples of this include: Perkins Engines, particularly for machine operators whose jobs have been de-skilled by technical change; Laing O'Rourke, whose unqualified building workers welcome the opportunity to gain an NVQ2; and BIGBORO, which reduces the effect on labour turnover of its low pay scales in IT services by offering upgrade training opportunities.

This evidence is broadly consistent with the expectation of a widely held employer preference for upgrade training over apprenticeship, given their implications for training costs, employee screening, and career motivation. These factors largely explain the predominance of upgrade training over apprenticeship in retailing and IT.

In other respects and in other circumstances, however, employers favour apprenticeship over upgrade training. Such is commonly the case in engineering and telecommunications, and to a lesser extent in construction.

One reason is that the cost of upgrade training can exceed that of apprenticeship. That is particularly likely when the job requires employees to have acquired extensive vocational knowledge in order to be fully productive. Upgrade training may be able to reach such skill levels only at excessive cost, if at all. Thus the four interviewees who state that upgrade training does not produce adequate levels of skill include two small-batch producers of sophisticated engineering equipment (Marshall Aerospace and STEAMCO) and one supplier of advanced construction services (NG Bailey). By contrast, J.C. Bamford, Siemens Standard Drives, and BT all use upgrade training extensively as a source of intermediate skills.

> 'Some employers...note that the cost of apprenticeship is reduced relative to upgrade training by the fact that it involves younger trainees...'

Some employers, including Rolls-Royce and NG Bailey, note that the cost of apprenticeship is reduced relative to upgrade training by the fact that it involves younger trainees, who are not only paid less but are also more willing to live away from home when their technical education requires that.

Wider benefits from apprenticeship are reported in some cases. The most striking is BT, which has attempted to quantify the benefits of apprenticeship relative to recruitment and upgrade training as sources of intermediate skills (Box 3).

> ### BOX 3 APPRENTICESHIP AS PART OF HUMAN RESOURCE STRATEGY: BT
>
> Created by the privatisation of British Telecom in 1984, BT rapidly shut down its predecessor's long-standing apprenticeship programme. During the deep cuts in employment, low quit rate, and low recruitment of the

ensuing 12 years, intermediate skills, primarily those of field service engineers and IT technicians, were obtained by short courses of upgrade training for less skilled employees. The decisions to restart apprenticeship (in 1996) and subsequently to make it the main source of additions to skilled workforce reflected two factors. The first was a desire to inject 'new blood' into the workforce. The second was an internal 'business case', which concluded that taking on an apprentice rather than an experienced adult increased profits by £1,300 a year, as a result partly of access to public funding. No effect on labour turnover is mentioned. Apprenticeship is nowadays an important component of the company's HR strategy.

Some employers, including Siemens Standard Drives, see apprenticeship as facilitating labour turnover, and favour upgrade training accordingly. But several see apprenticeship as superior to upgrade training in terms of labour turnover. This may be because upgrade training can itself facilitate movement between employers, as experienced by McNicholas and LogicaCMG Outsourcing.

> '...apprenticeship...may do more to develop loyalty to the company, and consequently reduce labour turnover.'

A second consideration is apprenticeship's effect on labour turnover. Even when apprenticeship objectively improves trainees' outside employment options more than does upgrade training, it may also develop loyalty to the company, and consequently reduce labour turnover. Perkins Engines, STEAMCO, both local authorities, Morrison, NG Bailey, Bells Stores, two out of the three Co-ops, Pilot Outlet, and BT Global all depict apprenticeship as either an actual or an expected source of lower labour turnover. And LogicaCMG Outsourcing may begin an apprenticeship programme in the future partly because that would be expected to reduce the company's quit rate.

Two mechanisms are reported for any favourable effect of apprenticeship on labour turnover. The first is the scope it offers the employer for the selection and socialisation of early prospects for long-term employment. The second is the explicit linking of apprenticeship to educational progression and career advancement within the company.

The substantial number of cases in which apprenticeship is seen as reducing losses of skilled labour indicates the extent to which apprenticeship can dovetail with wider HR strategies. It suggests also that the difference between apprenticeship and upgrade training, in terms of their compatibility with those strategies, may not only be smaller than expected but may also favour apprenticeship more widely than expected.

Indeed, upgrade training and apprenticeship are sometimes viewed as complements rather than substitutes. Employers who operate both types of training include Marshall Aerospace, whose training manager values its youth training (under Advanced

Apprenticeship) on the ground that it provides the 'seed-corn for the future' and its adult training on the ground that 'you can't buy maturity'. The company's two programmes are effectively both apprenticeships, but the point would apply even were the adult one confined to upgrade training.

> '...upgrade training and apprenticeship are sometimes viewed as complements rather than substitutes.'

Finally, the greater importance of upgrade training relative to apprenticeship in some cases is a by-product of the organisation's recent history. Some employers have begun to provide apprenticeships only recently. The contribution of apprenticeship to their skilled employment can be expected to rise, as older cohorts of skilled employees retire and are replaced by the younger ones containing ex-apprentices.

CONCLUSIONS

Apprenticeship is used only selectively and partially by large employers to meet their demand for intermediate skills. This reflects the competing attractions of recruitment and upgrade training, insofar as they function as alternative sources of skill. Even where apprenticeship is used, its role is typically shared with one or both alternatives, and it rarely accounts for a majority of the skilled workforce.

> '...apprenticeship...rarely accounts for a majority of the skilled workforce.'

The appeal of apprenticeship hinges primarily on two factors, both associated with the HR strategies pursued by large employers. The first is the limitations of recruitment, in terms of low and unreliable labour quality, low adaptability to the particular employer's 'way', and a high propensity to quit. If the employer's labour requirements vary strongly over time or place, however, recruitment is typically the preferred option.

The second factor favouring apprenticeship – or at least not penalising it as heavily as in the past – is its adaptation to the same HR strategies. The potentially sharp distinction between it and upgrade training – in terms of training cost, employee screening, career progression, adaptation to employer culture, effect on labour turnover, and the overall threat to the employer's investment in skills – is in some cases weak, in others reversed. Apprenticeship is indeed typically more expensive and more geared to external skill standards than is upgrade training. The differences between the two have, however, shrunk, particularly in the newer sectors of retailing and IT. Several employers see apprenticeship as creating superior outcomes, in terms of employee skills, attitudes, motivation and loyalty. The content of Advanced Apprenticeships can nowadays be matched closely to particular employers' requirements. These factors have facilitated the increasing incorporation of apprenticeship into mainstream HR practice – and, by the same token, encouraged employers to use it as a source of intermediate skills.

APPRENTICESHIP OUTSIDE THE FORMAL 3
APPRENTICESHIP PROGRAMME

❖ **Our cases suggest that large employers offer little apprenticeship outside Advanced Apprenticeship programmes**

❖ **The distinction between 'apprenticeship' and 'Apprenticeship' is nevertheless important, especially as the Government's usage confuses the issue**

❖ **Where employers are avoiding Advanced Apprenticeship, it is usually because of public funding problems or ineligibility of participants rather than because of aversion to the scheme**

INTRODUCTION

The importance attributed to Advanced Apprenticeship in sustaining the notion of 'apprenticeship' overall depends partly on the extent to which some form of apprenticeship still functions without the formal programme's support.

Some strands of evidence have suggested that what we term here 'non-AA apprenticeship' has been, and may still be, a substantial phenomenon. In 1994, when Modern Apprenticeship was still at the pilot stage, in responses to household surveys more than 200,000 people identified themselves as apprentices (Leman and Williams, 1995). Four years later, when Modern Apprenticeship had grown substantially, 16–24-year-olds who classed themselves

as 'apprentices' still outnumbered registered participants by three to two (Ryan and Unwin, 2001). More recently, as shown in Table 6, one in five respondents to a survey of the CIPD's membership reported that their employer provides 'apprenticeship-type training outside of government initiatives'.

The remit of the LSC's National Contracts Service (NCS) also suggests that some large employers may provide apprenticeship-type training outside the formal Apprenticeship programme. The NCS seeks to persuade more large employers to participate in the Apprenticeships programme. Although its 'hit list' of large, non-participating employers is not publicly available, the numbers

Table 6 ❖ Apprenticeship-related activities of CIPD members		
		% of respondents
Aware of Advanced Apprenticeship	Aware and involved	20
	Aware and not involved	57
	Not aware	23
Provide non-AA apprenticeship[1]	Yes	21
	No	68
	Don't know	11
Role in AA (if involved)	Sole sponsor	48
	Joint sponsor	17
	Subcontractor	18
	Other	17

Source: CIPD Training and Development Survey, 2005

Notes: 1. Responses to the question 'Does your organisation have any involvement with apprenticeship-type training outside of Government initiatives (for instance, programmes for craft and technician level that contain both on-the-job training and off-the-job technical instruction)?'

involved appear to be substantial. Although we do not expect most non-participating employers to provide bespoke apprenticeships, some may well do so.

The evidence available to date is, however, only suggestive. Further investigation of the issue is therefore desirable.

IMPLEMENTATION

In pursuing evidence of non-AA apprenticeship, we use the definitions outlined in Chapter 1. In particular, 'apprenticeship' denotes all Level 3–4 training programmes that combine on-the-job training and off-the-job vocational learning, irrespective of whether they are formally called 'apprenticeship' and whether they are funded through the Advanced Apprenticeships programme.

We therefore class as 'apprenticeship' any training programme that meets the criterion, whether or not that label is attached to it. Adults taking part in training programmes that satisfy the criterion are classed as apprentices, whether or not they are called that. All Advanced Apprenticeship programmes are classed as apprenticeship, even where there are doubts about the status of their Technical Certificates as technical education – as, notably, in retailing.

Our definition excludes the rest of the Apprenticeships programme – here termed other (or Foundation) Apprenticeships – as it is geared to Level 2 skills. The distinction is particularly difficult to implement in construction. In that sector nowadays, training for some core trades, including bricklaying and painting, is largely confined to Level 2 qualifications, and Apprentices aiming at Level 3 ones first complete a common Level 2 programme.

Nor do we class as apprenticeship any programme that uses the name but does not meet the criterion – such as one retailer's 'team-leader apprenticeship' programme, which lacks off-the-job instruction and a Technical Certificate.

> '...the distinction between apprenticeship and upgrade training is blurred around the edges.'

We treat as upgrade training two types of programme for adult employees. The first type contains no technical education – for instance, Bells Stores' adult programme, which is confined to work-based learning and the associated NVQ3. The second type includes some technical education but involves specialised production work rather than departmental rotation during learning – as at J.C. Bamford and Siemens Standard Drives (Box 2, page 11). These two cases remind us that, as noted in the previous chapter, the distinction between apprenticeship and upgrade training is blurred around the edges.

EXTENT OF NON-AA APPRENTICESHIP

To what extent does apprenticeship function nowadays outside the Apprenticeships programme? We would not expect any employer who employs intermediate skills in new Advanced Apprenticeship occupations, including retailing and IT, to have developed apprenticeship outside the Apprenticeship

programme. We therefore treat the question as relevant only to the sectors that were involved in apprenticeship before Modern Apprenticeship arrived, as represented here by engineering, construction, and telecommunications, and elsewhere by road transport, hairdressing, and printing.

A distinction must be drawn between apprenticeship programmes whose employer-providers decline to participate in Apprenticeships even though their programmes are eligible, and programmes that are simply ineligible for LSC funding. The two categories are termed 'eligible but outside' and 'ineligible and outside' respectively.

Eligible but outside

Concerning the first category, the answer to the question 'How much non-AA apprenticeship is there?' appears to be 'Not much' for engineering and telecommunications, and 'none' for construction, among large employers at least. Many employers are indeed critical of various attributes of the Apprenticeships programme and some do not participate as a result. But the non-participants whom we encountered do not generally operate apprenticeships with non-AA designs, whether developed by themselves or inherited from their sector's tradition.

The principal exception among our cases is the traineeship programme for field service engineers provided by Siemens Traffic Controls (Box 4). The programme meets the criterion for apprenticeship, but it is not supported by Advanced Apprenticeship, and its eligibility for support is not clear, given the lack of any directly relevant Advanced Apprenticeship framework.

BOX 4 NON-AA APPRENTICESHIP: SIEMENS TRAFFIC CONTROLS

One of this division's leading activities is the manufacture, installation, and maintenance of road traffic equipment in the UK. Most employees with intermediate skills are field service engineers, dispersed around the country. Until recently these skills were obtained entirely by recruitment and upgrade training. In 2001 the company established a 'traineeship' programme in urban traffic signals engineering, which now lasts three years. It comprises annual residential courses at the company's training centre, day release to local colleges for ONC and HND studies, and a broad training curriculum. Most entrants are 16–17-year-olds with five GCSE subjects at grades A–C.

On our criterion, the traineeship constitutes an apprenticeship. The company does not use the term itself, as it wishes to differentiate the programme both from low-quality traditional apprenticeship and from the Advanced Apprenticeship programme. The traineeships remain outside Advanced Apprenticeship partly because of the absence of a suitable training framework, and partly because a previous Modern Apprenticeship programme for manufacturing test engineers, organised by external providers, had been discontinued as a result of a low completion rate.

Within our case studies we encountered no other instance of voluntary non-AA apprenticeship. The closest approximation is the graduate training programme at Data Connection, which the company would want to keep outside Advanced Apprenticeship, even were funding to become available, in order to be able to operate the programme according to its own requirements.

> 'Further Education colleges do not offer courses in specialist fields when only a few learners are involved.'

A further reason for non-participation in the formal Apprenticeship programme is the absence of accessible provision for technical education in general and recognised Technical Certificates in particular. Further Education colleges do not offer courses in specialist fields when only a few learners are involved. Many private providers are not capable of providing technical education (as opposed to Key Skills training and assessment) for the training frameworks whose Technical Certificates require it.

The large firms that face this difficulty include those whose skilled employees are scattered around the country, notably at BT Retail and Siemens Traffic Controls in telecommunications. Both employers do, however, possess the resources and the willingness to incur what are substantial costs for centralising their off-the-job training and technical education at a single Further Education college or company training centre, delivered on a 'residential block release' basis. BT has opted to bring its programme under Advanced Apprenticeship; Siemens Traffic Controls, to remain outside.

Some smaller employers and some less well-resourced ones, including some convenience stores operators in retailing, react to the unavailability of suitable courses at local colleges by avoiding Apprenticeships altogether. By the same token, in the absence of technical education, any training they sponsor will not constitute 'apprenticeship' either.

There is only one case to report in terms of non-AA apprenticeship resulting from a decision by a large employer to train along apprenticeship lines but to remain outside the programme.

Ineligible and outside

More non-AA apprenticeship is found in the second category: training programmes that the employer would like to, but cannot, bring under Advanced Apprenticeship.

The reasons for ineligibility are varied. The first is again the lack of a suitable training framework. This factor might contribute to the absence of apprenticeship at McNicholas, with its requirement for specialist skills in street works. Outside the ranks of large employers, we heard of smaller, specialist employers in such specialties as roofing, scaffolding, and narrow-boat building who train young people outside Apprenticeships because of the absence of a suitable training framework. The status of such programmes as 'apprenticeship' may, however, be jeopardised by lack of any technical education content.

More visibly, some case-study employers who participate in Apprenticeships also provide apprenticeships that do not come under the programme. In some cases the training is the same as under Advanced Apprenticeship, but particular categories of participant cannot be funded by the LSC and therefore do not come under the Apprenticeship programme. The principal ones are graduates, adults, and technicians.

> '...no individual should enjoy two bites of the cherry, in terms of public funding for post-secondary learning.'

Graduate programmes are not eligible for LSC funding even when their content conforms to a framework recognised for Apprenticeship. (The rationale is that no individual should enjoy two bites of the cherry, in terms of public funding for post-secondary learning.) Thus, while craft apprentices at STEAMCO come under Advanced Apprenticeship, graduate trainees, who receive what is in effect a graduate apprenticeship, and some of whom go into technician and assistant professional work, do not. Similarly, Data Connection's graduate programme is organised as upgrade training, but, even were it reorganised as apprenticeship, it would remain ineligible for public funding, as all recruits have a first degree.

A similar situation applies to adult apprenticeships. Although adults became eligible in 2004 in principle for public funding under Apprenticeships, the funds available have made possible only small pilot programmes in a few localities. Consequently, adult apprentices at Rolls-Royce (Derby), Marshall Aerospace, Leicester City Council's Maintenance DSO and BT Global (Box 5), who receive training similar or identical to that of their youth counterparts, are not supported by Advanced Apprenticeship. The same applies to the 10% or less of apprentices who enter at age 25 or older in the programmes operated by Laing O'Rourke, Morrison, and Mowlem Building South West.

BOX 5 ADULT APPRENTICESHIP: ROLLS-ROYCE (DERBY) AND LEICESTER CITY COUNCIL'S MAINTENANCE DIRECT SERVICES ORGANISATION

Rolls-Royce (Derby) and Leicester City Council Maintenance DSO both train as many adults (25+ yrs) as youths in their craft apprenticeship programmes. These employers' training costs are higher for adults than for youths, as adults are not eligible for Advanced Apprenticeship support and (at Rolls-Royce) their pay is higher than that of young apprentices.

The two organisations differ in the types of adult they train and the principal reason for training adults. Rolls-Royce extended apprenticeship training to less skilled adult employees in the early 1990s in order to avoid compulsory redundancies. It continued the practice in response to widespread employee demand. The principal trade union, having agreed to the access of less skilled adults to skilled work, pressed for the same content of training for adults as for young apprentices.

Leicester CC's Maintenance DSO, which maintains the Council's residential housing, fills around half the places on its five-year, multi-skilled apprenticeship programme with adults, all recruited externally. The choice of a large adult component reflects the Council's social objectives, including equality of opportunity by age.

The third category marked by widespread ineligibility is technician apprenticeship. As for adults, the problem is one of funding availability rather than of principle. Technician apprenticeships are formally eligible for public funding, but the responsibility for Level 4 programmes nowadays falls to the Higher Education Funding Council (HEFCE), not to the LSC, whose predecessor funded both technician and craft-level apprenticeships. Engineering employers whose apprenticeship programmes include technician as well as craft trainees report little success for efforts to obtain public funding from the HEFCE. They see the HEFCE as more concerned to support full-time post-secondary education in general, and Foundation Degrees in particular, than apprenticeship. Their account is consistent with the content of the HEFCE website, which provides (at the time of writing) no readily accessible evidence of financial support for technician apprenticeships and the HNC and HND qualifications with which they have traditionally been associated. The development of work-based Foundation Degrees may change that, but in the meantime what remains of technician apprenticeship not only stands outside Apprenticeship but also receives little public support.

A final source of involuntary exclusion of apprenticeships from Advanced Apprenticeship involves not any ineligibility in principle but rather the limited amount of funds that the LSC has at its disposal. None of our interviewees said that they would have liked to recruit more Advanced Apprentices than the LSC was prepared to support, but one related that this has been the case for another organisation.

Similarly, some apprenticeship may have suffered from a refusal by an LSC to support particular providers. One of our retail co-operative case studies reported that its local LSC had threatened to withdraw its Apprenticeships contract on the ground that programmes with fewer than 50 participants would no longer be accepted. The threat proved empty in that instance, but it may not have done so for other employers.

In all these instances, therefore, the 'non-AA' status of the apprenticeships in question arises from lack of access to public funding, rather than from any aversion to Advanced Apprenticeship on the part of the employer.

CONCLUSIONS

Although other evidence has suggested that a significant amount of apprenticeship exists outside the Advanced Apprenticeship programme, we have found only limited evidence of it among large employers in our four training 'sectors'. Moreover, where it does exist, it is primarily involuntary, associated with the ineligibility of particular categories of participant (graduates, adults) and of particular levels of training (technician, assistant professional) for funding by the LSC under the rules and practices that it uses to administer Apprenticeships.

Only one instance was encountered of a large employer whose apprenticeship programme is potentially eligible to participate in Apprenticeship but who has decided to go it alone. There may be others. Nevertheless, as far as apprenticeship goes, we conclude that 'it's almost all Advanced Apprenticeship now'. Apprenticeship does exist outside the Advanced Apprenticeship programme, but that reflects primarily ineligibility or funding limitations rather than bespoke programme designs.

The existence of a considerable amount of involuntary non-AA apprenticeships does, however, underline the importance of the distinction between 'apprenticeship' and 'Apprenticeship'. From the policy standpoint, the need for such a distinction arises partly from the confusion caused by the Government's decision to use the term 'apprenticeship' for all work-based training funded by the LSC, including that aimed only at Level 2 skills. The case is reinforced by the ineligibility for support under the Apprenticeship programme of particular categories of apprentice and apprenticeship. Yet more confusion would have been avoided had the Government not decided to use the generic term 'apprenticeship', unaccompanied by the qualifier 'modern', as the brand name for its Level 3 youth training programmes.

From the standpoint of HR managers, the question for those interested in using apprenticeship is whether the advantage of the public subsidies that come with Advanced Apprenticeship outweighs the disadvantages of the programme's less attractive features, such as increased administrative cost. The next chapter discusses this issue in detail.

EMPLOYER PARTICIPATION IN ADVANCED APPRENTICESHIP: PRESENCE

4

❖ **Employer participation in Advanced Apprenticeship remains partial overall, and highly variable across sectors**

❖ **Participation depends in part on how the employer evaluates the vocational learning content of Advanced Apprenticeship**

❖ **The appeal of Advanced Apprenticeship depends on the context**

INTRODUCTION

The next issue is the extent to which large employers participate in the Advanced Apprenticeship programme, and why they do or do not do so.

The lack of 'household name' employers in lists of Apprenticeship providers has suggested widespread non-participation by very large employers in particular. As outlined in Chapter 1, such evidence has caused concern among policy-makers, leading to efforts to establish the nature of the problem and to increase participation by large employers.

Three aspects of employer participation are considered: presence, scale and intensity, and content. They are discussed in turn in this and the following two chapters.

PATTERNS

> 'Participation appears to be considerable in construction, engineering, and telecommunications...'

The first issue is whether employers participate in Advanced Apprenticeship or not. The case studies suggest that the situation differs considerably across sectors. Participation appears to be considerable in construction, engineering, and telecommunications, sectors with well-established training frameworks. It is moderate but uneven in retailing, and only marginal in IT – sectors in which apprenticeship is a recent development.

In construction, almost all of the case-study employers train Apprentices, of whom a minority typically goes on to Advanced

Apprenticeships. The sole case-study employer that does not currently participate states an intention to start doing so this year.

Most engineering and telecommunications cases, both those we studied in detail and those whom we contacted but did not pursue, participate in Advanced Apprenticeships. Most operate long-standing apprenticeship programmes, which they brought under Modern Apprenticeship in its early days. The category includes BT, J.C. Bamford, Marshall Aerospace, Rolls-Royce, and STEAMCO.

The three employers in those sectors that do not participate span the range of alternatives. One prefers recruitment to training (PARTSCO). One opts for upgrade training rather than apprenticeship (Siemens Standard Drives). The third has not sought to bring its apprenticeships under the Apprenticeships programme (Siemens Traffic Controls).

Retailing occupies an intermediate position. In four of the nine cases, the employer provides Advanced Apprenticeships. Those employers include the operators of convenience stores operators (Bells Stores and the three distribution sector co-ops), but no operators of department stores.

IT sits at the other pole. No case-study employer provides Advanced Apprenticeships; only one, BIGBORO's IT services, offers (Foundation) Apprenticeships.

FACTORS

The reasons case-study employers do or do not use apprenticeship in general, as discussed in Chapter 2, overlap, by definition, with the reasons they do or do not participate in Advanced Apprenticeship. The factors common to both decisions include, for example, whether the employer's demand for skill centres on Level 3, as opposed to above that, at Level 4–5, as in much of IT services, or below it, at Level 2, as in most construction and retailing employment.

We concentrate here on the two particular aspects: the broader factors associated with employers' attitudes to apprenticeship, and specific attributes of the Apprenticeships programme itself.

Product market: intermediate goods

The contextual factors start with one that the engineering case studies suggest is important, in manufacturing at least: whether a company produces intermediate or final goods and services. The two employers in that sector that do not provide engineering apprenticeships, PARTSCO and Siemens Standard Drives, both produce intermediate goods for large customers' supply chains. Two of those who provide apprenticeships produce final products (J.C. Bamford and Rolls-Royce, Derby). One produces intermediate products, but they account for a large share of the value of the final product (Perkins Engines).

> 'Even though the parent company typically helps raise productivity and cut prices, the pressure to minimise costs bears heavily on how intermediate skills are acquired.'

Competition is notoriously intense, on both price and quality, in markets for intermediate goods. Large buyers, led by the parent company, demand continuous price reductions. Even though the parent company typically helps raise productivity and cut prices, the pressure to minimise costs bears heavily on how intermediate skills are acquired. PARTSCO chose its location partly because of the district's high rate of skilled unemployment. Siemens Standard Drives uses upgrade training to reduce the cost of skills acquisition relative to that under apprenticeship (Box 2, page 11).

Product market: convenience and department stores

Retailers who operate many small convenience stores tend to participate in Advanced Apprenticeship, whereas those who operate department stores tend not to do so (Box 6). The difference in participation between the two sub-sectors may reflect that in their product markets.

BOX 6 CONVENIENCE STORES AND DEPARTMENT STORES: IPSWICH AND NORWICH CO-OPERATIVE SOCIETY, AND JOHN LEWIS AND SELFRIDGES

The facilities operated by Ipswich and Norwich Co-op are primarily convenience stores. Ipswich and Norwich provides Advanced Apprenticeships in retailing. John Lewis and Selfridges operate large department stores.

Neither participates in Advanced Apprenticeship.

Convenience store retailers find it hard to recruit and then retain experienced store managers. Although young people with an aptitude for and an interest in store management are also scarce, those trained via Advanced Apprenticeship have proved relatively stable and effective. The supervisory requirements of Level 3 NVQs, which discourage other employers, as frequently in construction, from using youth apprenticeships, actually suit employers in a sector in which young employees can become deputy store managers by age 21.

The department store retailers, who offer higher pay and potentially better career prospects, enjoy a wider choice of employees for such intermediate level roles as team leader and section manager. The importance of developing the company's corporate image and culture, and of personality traits such as maturity and reliability in dealing with customers, results in a preference for adult rather than youth training, and for bespoke upgrade training rather than apprenticeship.

A further factor may be the greater development of the HR function in department store than in convenience store retailing, which encourages the former type of employer to tailor its own programmes but discourages the latter type from doing so. The practices of the convenience store operations of large supermarket chains, such as Tesco and Sainsbury, with their well-resourced HR functions, are potentially informative here.

Labour market: collective regulation and customer requirements

The participation of construction employers in Apprenticeship is encouraged by external regulation. The most striking instance concerns electrical contracting, in which health and safety regulation and an active sectoral joint body have sustained high levels of training and apprenticeship (Gospel and Druker, 1998). Two more recent developments also encourage more training: the spread of the Construction Skills Certification Scheme and pressure on subcontractors to show evidence of appropriate workforce qualifications. The immediate effect is increased upgrade training for adult employees, to Level 2 in particular, but indirect effects on youth training to Level 3 are apparent in one large building firm (Box 7).

BOX 7 PUBLIC REGULATION, CLIENT REQUIREMENTS, AND EMPLOYEE SKILLS: LAING O'ROURKE LEARNING WORLD

The incentive to building firm employers to provide training in construction has been increased by two developments. The first is the spread of the Construction

Skills Certification Scheme, which seeks to have all workers on building sites qualified to at least NVQ Level 2. The second is increasing demands by large clients that their main subcontractors demonstrate a high level of qualifications in their workforces – including those of secondary subcontractors and the self-employed. Laing O'Rourke has responded to these developments with a plan to use Learning World, the joint venture from which it sources its training programmes, to revitalise what has in recent years dwindled into a marginal apprenticeship programme.

National origins

'Foreign ownership is a further potential influence on participation.'

Foreign ownership is a further potential influence on participation. We included particular types of foreign-owned employer, with a view to identifying companies that specialise in either upgrade training or non-AA apprenticeship. Japanese and German ownership were seen as potentially conducive to upgrade training and non-AA apprenticeship respectively.

The results diverged from expectation. The two Japanese-owned cases intentionally rely on recruitment as the primary source of intermediate skills. Of the two German-owned cases, both Siemens subsidiaries, one focuses on upgrade training, in association with its 'Japanese production methods' approach to manufacturing. The other does provide non-AA apprenticeships, as outlined in Chapter 3, but without any manifest link to German apprenticeship. None of the four companies reports that its decisions reflect any shortage of suitably qualified potential apprentices in the UK.

'These cases...underline the extent to which HR decision-making is decentralised within multinational companies, and to which pragmatism dominates the decisions of overseas divisions and subsidiaries.'

These cases are therefore consistent with the dominance of 'host country' over 'home country' effects in setting HR practices. They also underline the extent to which HR decision-making is decentralised within multinational companies, and to which pragmatism dominates the decisions of overseas divisions and subsidiaries (Ferner, 1997; Almond et al, 2005).

Trade unions

Trade unions appear to be only a marginal influence on the choice between the two types of training – largely because they are not always present, but also because, even when they are present, most interviewees see them as having little or no influence on training decisions. Several employers report union support for training in general and for apprenticeship in particular. The only cases that suggest any substantial union influence are two that favoured apprenticeship. One is Rolls-Royce (Derby), where trade unions pressed successfully for adult trainees to receive the same training as apprentices. The other is Leicester Council DSO, where the council's preference for a high-quality, five-year apprenticeship programme matches that of the unions it recognises.

Public relations

Finally, public relations may be important, although the extent is difficult to gauge. Larger employers are more likely to experience external pressure to participate in a high-profile government programme, and to do so even if on purely economic criteria they might opt not to do so. The issue is a sensitive one, difficult to explore in one-off interviews, but some patterns suggest its relevance – including the 'pilot' Advanced Apprenticeship programmes that three employers in construction and retailing are either running or considering at present.

'Considerations related to corporate social responsibility are particularly likely to affect high-profile large companies in general...'

Similarly, the training manager of one engineering employer states that the company's participation in Advanced Apprenticeship probably means more to the government than the programme means to the company. PARTSCO, which relies entirely on recruitment for Level 3 skills, enjoys a low public profile, which may have helped the company avoid drawing attention to its non-participation in the Apprenticeships programme. Considerations related to corporate social responsibility are particularly likely to affect high-profile large companies in general, and those for which central government is a leading customer, including some engineering firms, in particular.

The influence of public relations must, however, be limited. Several prominent employers in IT and retailing have not only remained outside the programme but have also indicated that their willingness to participate depends on the modification of the programme's requirements to make in-house training programmes acceptable largely without modification. In such cases, the mountain is required to come to Mahomet, and, as we show in Chapter 7, it seems increasingly willing to do so.

ATTRIBUTES OF APPRENTICESHIPS

The decision to provide Advanced Apprenticeships is expected to depend also on how the employer views the programme's incentives and requirements.

We start with the employer's overall assessment of the programme's success. A close association is apparent in the case studies between the decision to participate and the verdict on

Table 7 Attributes of Advanced Apprenticeship as evaluated by case-study employers				
	Influence on participation (number of respondents)			Correlation with participation[b]
	negative	neutral	positive	
NVQ Level 3–4	8	6	14	0.37
Technical Certificate	7	6	15	0.36
Effect on labour turnover	1	10	14	0.31
Administrative requirements	19	7	2	0.16
Inspection requirements and findings	7	12	8	0.14
Programme's reputation	5	14	8	0.13
Better-quality employees	0	9	18	0.05
Key Skills	10	7	10	0.00
Help young people	0	5	23	0.01
Encouraged by other bodies[a]	2	14	12	-0.01
Encouraged by trade union(s)	0	23	5	-0.01
Public funding (cuts training costs)	0	7	21	-0.13
Effect on your public image	0	9	18	-0.22
Expect frequent change in programme requirements	16	9	1	-0.01

Notes: a. Learning and Skills Council, Sector Skills Council, employer's association, Chamber of Commerce
b. Pearson correlation with actual participation in Advanced Apprenticeship

AA's success. Fifteen of the thirty employers currently participate in Advanced Apprenticeship in the chosen occupations. Those who give a verdict on the success of the programme all rate it as successful – eight 'highly' so, seven 'moderately' so. Of those who do not participate, two disqualified themselves as not adequately informed, and another six answered the same question, only one of whom rated the programme successful.

Turning to the programme's detailed attributes, interviewees who judged themselves to be in a position to answer were presented with a series of attributes and asked whether they see them as a positive, neutral, or negative influence on their decision concerning participation. The fourteen attributes are listed in Table 7 above.

Favoured attributes

The factors that are evaluated most favourably, whether or not the organisation participates, are, in descending order: helping young people, reducing training costs by drawing on public funding, and improving the organisation's public image. With regards to the first attribute the results are unsurprising – few could reject the desirability in principle of helping young people – but that is less likely for the second and third ones. The share of interviewees who see public funding as an attraction is highest in ICT, the 'sector' with the lowest participation rate. Similarly, some organisations that do not participate see that there would be potential benefits for public relations, were they to participate.

The next most attractive factors concern the issues discussed in Chapter 2: the effect on labour turnover, for which only one employer sees negative effects, and access to better-quality employees, with ability, qualifications, and motivation as the

attributes that our interviewees suggest. The contribution of Advanced Apprenticeship to employee quality is seen as favourable by most interviewees in all sectors except engineering. In that sector most interviewees see the programme as making no difference, primarily because they view their Apprenticeships as simply a repackaging of the apprenticeships they would provide anyway. No employer sees it as worsening employee quality.

> 'The contribution of Advanced Apprenticeship to employee quality is seen as favourable by most interviewees in all sectors except engineering.'

Also favourably evaluated overall, but with more indifference and more disagreement than for turnover and employee quality, are two components of the Apprenticeship training frameworks themselves: the NVQ certificate for work-based learning and the Technical Certificate for 'underpinning knowledge'.

Employers who react adversely to NVQs are mostly found in the sectors with apprenticeship traditions – engineering, construction, and telecommunications – in which the critics of NVQs are as numerous as their supporters. In retailing, none of the interviewees finds NVQs a negative factor – although that cannot be expected to apply across the sector as a whole.

The response to Technical Certificates is almost uniformly favourable in engineering and telecommunications, mostly favourable in construction, mostly neutral in IT, and mostly adverse (four out of eight responses) in retailing.

Disfavoured attributes

The attributes that discourage participation are few, but widely disliked: administrative requirements – the term 'bureaucracy' is used by many interviewees – and an expectation of frequent changes in requirements, including the content of training frameworks. The latter is viewed almost universally as a negative factor in retailing and IT, the new apprenticeship sectors, but responses are mixed in engineering, construction, and telecommunications, the long-standing sectors.

Neutral attributes

> 'Criticism of the Key Skills requirement is widespread.'

Criticism of the Key Skills requirement is widespread. The objections are familiar: the additional time and cost involved, the hostility to it of most Apprentices, and an assertion of the Government's responsibility for developing Key Skills in compulsory education. Nevertheless, the responses show considerable dispersion. Several employers accept the Key Skills component and some go out of their way to persuade Apprentices of the need to learn those skills, for example, as future convenience store managers who will need to know how to handle numbers and write reports. Others manage to integrate the teaching, though not the assessment, of Key Skills into the NVQ or the Technical Certificate.

The net result is a near-neutral balance of employer opinion on Key Skills. Positive ratings are particularly widespread in engineering, where skill requirements are high and most Apprentices have sufficient recent GCSEs or A Levels to be exempt from the core Key Skills requirement. By contrast, no construction employer sees Key Skills as encouraging it to participate, and four view it as a deterrent.

Employer opinion is also divided over the requirement for the external inspection of their training provision. Several employers said they welcome the external feedback and advice that inspection provides. Favourable or neutral reactions are the norm in engineering and construction; adverse ones, in retailing. In each of the former two sectors, however, the manager of a long-established apprenticeship programme faults the external inspection that its company has experienced for a lack of sectoral expertise and the use of inappropriate criteria – notably an emphasis on procedure rather than content. Several employers see some mix of additional paperwork and the duplication of effort in response to multiple inspection bodies as discouraging participation in Apprenticeships.

Attributes and employer participation

Such are the views of employers. But which attributes actually matter when it comes to deciding whether or not to participate in

Advanced Apprenticeship? The final column of Table 7 indicates that employers' evaluations of most attributes of Advanced Apprenticeships are not closely associated with the outcomes of their participation decisions. The two exceptions concern the NVQ and the Technical Certificate components of training frameworks. Employers who say that those factors have encouraged them to participate are more likely to participate than those who view the same factors unfavourably.

The programme's expected effect on labour turnover, which is mostly viewed as favourable, is also associated with participation. Employers who see it as a potentially important influence on participation more commonly participate than those who do not. This tendency aligns with the evidence in chapter 2 concerning the selective integration of Advanced Apprenticeship into employers' HR strategies.

> 'Paradoxically, the availability of public funding under Advanced Apprenticeship and its effect on the organisation's public image...are negatively associated with participation itself...'

Paradoxically, the availability of public funding under Advanced Apprenticeship and its effect on the organisation's public image, both of which are rated by most employers as a reason to participate, are negatively associated with participation itself – although not closely. This suggests that, although several non-participants find these aspects attractive, that is not enough to outweigh the unattractive aspects. In a small non-random sample, however, the conclusion can only be tentative.

Also noteworthy is the absence of anycorrelation between the participation decision, on the one side, and the evaluation of the Key Skills requirement, the external inspection requirement, and the administrative burden, on the other. In the case of Key Skills, that reflects a broadly neutral balance of employer opinion. In the case of inspection and administration, however, although most interviewees report that these factors discourage participation, actual participation patterns do not directly relate to those attributes.

A further attribute was volunteered by a number of interviewees: the requirement to demonstrate supervisory experience in order to gain a work-based qualification (NVQ) from Level 3 upwards. Criticism on this score is particularly widespread in construction and retailing. Many in construction see it as impractical for teenagers to gain supervisory experience on building sites, given the hazards of the workplace and the challenges of the social environment. In retailing, convenience store employers tend to welcome the supervisory component, but even there some employers would like to be able to insert at least a year of work experience between ending Level 2 and starting the Level 3 NVQ without facing some loss of public funding for Level 3 training. The pause would permit teenage Apprentices to mature more before taking on supervisory work.

CONCLUSIONS

The evidence suggests that employer involvement in Advanced Apprenticeship remains partial overall, and highly variable across employers and sectors.

The case studies suggest that participation depends on how the employer evaluates the vocational learning content of Advanced Apprenticeship, as reflected in the appeal or otherwise of the vocational qualifications (NVQ, Technical Certificate). A further influence is whether participation is expected to reduce labour turnover. By contrast, the themes familiar in employers' complaints – Key Skills, and the burden of inspection and administration requirements – are not, in this sample at least, associated with the participation decision.

The appeal of Advanced Apprenticeship depends also on the context – notably the attributes of product and labour markets, sectoral skill requirements, and the factors that determine the relative appeal of recruitment and upgrade training, as discussed in Chapter 2.

EMPLOYER PARTICIPATION IN ADVANCED APPRENTICESHIP: SCALE AND INTENSITY

5

❖ **The scale and intensity of participation is limited and distinctly variable from employer to employer**

❖ **The limited number of apprentices reflects such features as the decentralisation of HR decisions, outsourcing of non-core activities, and, in some cases, protracted employment reduction**

INTRODUCTION

The second dimension of employers' participation in Advanced Apprenticeship is its scale. Although the Government emphasises the need to increase the number of participating employers, the number of Apprentices taken on by those who participate implicitly matters as well, in view of the targets adopted for the expansion of Apprenticeships and the decline in the number of Advanced Apprentices in the decade to date.

Two dimensions are relevant. The first is the absolute scale of participation: how many apprentices are trained? The second is intensity: how many apprentices are trained relative to employment in the occupations at which their training is aimed?

NUMBERS IN TRAINING

> 'The number of apprentices in training in our case studies is limited.'

The number of apprentices in training in our case studies is limited. Only four employers have more than 100 apprentices, even when non-AA ones are included. Compare this to the hundreds, in some cases thousands, of apprentices that could be found in large establishments in the first half of the last century – notably the 2,000-plus in training at both the Metropolitan-Vickers engineering factory in Manchester and the John Brown & Co. shipyard on the Clyde in the late 1930s, and the five engineering firms who had more than 1,000 apprentices in the late 1950s (Ryan, 2004; Liepmann, 1960). The changes in employment structure since then, in terms of sector and firm size, rule out a return to such activity levels, but a widespread increase in the size of apprentice programmes would be welcome.

Several factors account for the limited size of the apprentice programmes operated nowadays by large employers. The ensuing list is not exhaustive, as the factors associated with participation detailed in Chapter 4 are relevant here too. The first three factors concern the rapid restructuring of employment and management by many organisations.

Reorganisation: outsourcing

> 'Apprentice numbers are...restricted by the contracting-out of particular business functions.'

Apprentice numbers are in many cases restricted by the contracting-out of particular business functions. The organisation's employment is thereby reduced, and with it the absolute demand for intermediate skills. Training then depends more on the decisions of sub-contractors, who are mostly smaller firms, subject to more intense price competition, and more oriented to short-term profit than is the organisation doing the contracting-out. The training of apprentices for the activity as a whole is thereby reduced. In the building industry the Construction Skills Certification Scheme is intended to counter this problem.

Contracting-out is particularly extensive in construction, where several large employers have become in effect professional-service companies, concentrating on design and co-ordination functions and employing little or no production labour themselves. Our cases do not include any extreme examples, though Morrison's more extensive use of subcontracting in its

English than in its Scottish operations is a case in point.

Outsourcing is also extensive in heavy engineering, again particularly when site-based work is involved, as at STEAMCO. The same applies in IT services, where several large suppliers, including LogicaCMG Outsourcing, have benefited from the contracting out of IT functions by other large organisations, including central government departments.

Reorganisation: employment reduction

A factor that selectively depresses apprentice numbers is cutbacks in employment. Several of the engineering and telecommunications cases have experienced large falls in employment over the past two decades as a result of rapid technical change and high productivity growth. Their efforts to avoid compulsory redundancies, along with their low labour turnover rates, have meant little or no immediate need for fresh supplies of intermediate skills – and plenty of redundant employees to retrain, were the need to arise. In BT, the result was the suspension of apprentice intakes for 13 years. The revival of apprenticeship from 1996 onwards responded to the resulting age-related imbalance in the workforce.

Similarly, the reduction of skill requirements in production at Perkins Engines, associated with automation, along with low labour turnover, means that an apprentice intake of around 20 a year suffices to meet the company's non-cyclical skill requirements.

In retailing, by contrast, lower rates of technical change and productivity growth, along with expanding demand in the product market, have meant positive growth in skilled employment and upward pressure on apprentice intakes. The expansion plans currently in place at both Bells Stores and Ipswich & Norwich Co-op have sustained apprentice intakes of around 20 a year.

Reorganisation: decentralisation of HR decisions

A further damper on apprentice intakes applies when the unit to which HR decisions apply is itself small. Given the widespread decentralisation of training decisions within multi-division and multi-site organisations, it is necessary to distinguish between the size of the parent company and the size of the division or establishment. Some case studies are but one part of a larger organisation. Several are themselves only medium-sized, and employ only limited numbers in Level 3-4 roles. Such business units are typically allowed considerable discretion over their HR practices, including the choice of apprentice numbers.

> 'The difficulty of reaping economies of scale in training discourages the provision of apprenticeship...'

Such small to medium-sized business units typically do not need large numbers of apprentices in the first place. Some reject the idea of setting up an Advanced Apprenticeship programme on what could only be a small scale. The difficulty of reaping economies of scale in training discourages the provision of apprenticeship at PARTSCO and Data Connection in particular. The tendency has been intensified by the policy of some local LSCs, which is to deny contracts to providers who take only small numbers of Apprentices.

> 'Large employers in some sectors tend to centralise apprenticeship-related decisions.'

The situation differs in convenience store retailing and telecommunications, where the large number and small average size of local establishments make it impractical to devolve HR decisions to that level. Large employers in some sectors tend to centralise apprenticeship-related decisions. Similarly, in telecommunications, as for field services engineers at both BT and Siemens Traffic Controls, off-the-job training tends to be organised at a single location for all apprentices, who participate by way of residential block release.

INTENSITY

A simple measure of the scale of participation, which adjusts for the size of both the employer and its use of intermediate skills, is the number of apprentices relative to the number of skilled workers in the occupations for which the apprenticeship programme potentially qualifies them. This statistic, traditionally termed the apprentice–journeyman ratio, provides a useful indicator of the employer's training effort, the focus of interest here. It has the advantage of adjusting for the size of employment in intermediate skills. We calculate it for all apprentices, including adults, and not simply for those participating in Advanced Apprenticeship.

The ratio, expressed as a percentage, averages 7% across the 28 organisations for which it is available, and 11% for the 17 that provide apprenticeships (Table 8, opposite). On the latter basis, it averages 2% for the ICT cases, around 11% in engineering and retailing, and 16% in construction.

The variation across case studies is substantial. The organisations whose ratios for Level 3 apprentices exceed 30% are NG Bailey in construction and Ipswich & Norwich Co-op in retailing. By contrast, although Rolls-Royce (Derby) and BT both operate larger apprentice programmes, they have so many skilled employees that their intensity indices come out at less than 5%.

The contribution of apprenticeship to skill supplies therefore varies considerably by sector and employer according to the intensity of participation. The low intensity of participation by some large employers suggests room for expansion on the intensive margin (how many apprenticeships does the employer provide?), not just the extensive one (how many employers are involved?) on which public policy tends to focus.

Ownership and community ties

Differences in apprenticeship intensity across employers appear to be associated with several factors.

Table 8   Intensity of apprenticeship training of case-study employers (by sector and participation in Advanced Apprenticeship)

	Number of employers providing information	Intensity of apprenticeship training[a] (%)	
		All employers	Apprenticeship providers only
Engineering	7	8	11
Construction	6	14	16
Retailing	8	6	12
ICT	7	1	2
All	28	7	11

Notes: unweighted averages; two BT divisions counted separately
a. Number of apprentices (non-AA included) as a percentage of employment in the relevant occupation(s)

The first combines ownership structure and community ties. Some of the highest values for the intensity indicator are found in organisations that are not companies with dispersed ownership and that have strong and stable ties to a particular locality. This category includes companies with concentrated ownership (including family firms), non-profit organisations (including co-ops), and public sector bodies.

Examples of family-owned firms with high training intensity include J.C. Bamford, Marshall Aerospace, NG Bailey, and, until recently, Bells Stores. The first two also operate in a distinct local community (Burton and Cambridge, respectively). Bells Stores operates in the southern half of the north east. Other organisations that claim deep roots in a locality include Rolls-Royce in Derby, Perkins Engines in Peterborough, Leicester Council DSO and Ipswich & Norwich Co-op. The last three all have above-average apprentice training intensities.

Apprentice intensities tend to be lower in the 'stock market-owned' companies. The contrast between these two types of company suggests that concentrated ownership in general, and family ownership in particular, is associated with a larger apprentice training programme than is dispersed ownership – as in the difference between two aerospace engineering companies with roots in a particular locality (Box 8).

BOX 8 OWNERSHIP, COMMUNITY AND PRODUCT MARKETS: ROLLS-ROYCE (DERBY) AND MARSHALL AEROSPACE

Both of these aerospace companies produce high-technology engineering products and services. Both employ a highly skilled workforce. Both have a long and proud tradition of apprentice training. Both set up a parallel programme for adults in the 1990s. Both have deep roots in their home district (Derby and Cambridge, respectively), and both intend their training to serve local needs as well as their own.

The ownership structures of the companies are, however, different. Rolls-Royce is a quoted company with dispersed ownership. Marshall Aerospace is an unquoted, family-owned company, successive generations of whose owners have prioritised employee development and community service. The difference in ownership conditions, given similarly strong ties to the locality, is associated with a higher ratio of apprentices to craft-workers at Marshall Aerospace than at Rolls-Royce, at more than 10% and less than 5% respectively.

The difference in the companies' training intensities may also reflect other factors, including: recent and expected future changes in skilled employment; the greater size of Rolls-Royce, which may encourage a lower intensity of training; higher labour turnover at Marshall Aerospace, though the effect of that on training could go either way; and differences in products and skill needs between the large-batch production of new engines by Rolls-Royce, and the one-off or small-batch modification and repair of aircraft in service by Marshall Aerospace.

Such a pattern would be consistent with theories of corporate ownership and training, which depict companies with dispersed ownership as subject to pressure from the stock market to maximise reported earnings over short time periods, as opposed to over the longer term. One way to do so is to hold down expenditures on intangibles such as training, which, given their treatment in standard accounting practice as a current expense rather than an investment, increases reported earnings without worsening the balance sheet. Concentrated ownership potentially avoids such pressures. It also makes possible, depending on the objectives of the owners, a longer-term perspective on business success and greater investment in employee skills (Hall and Soskice, 2001).

The hypothesised role of financial considerations is consistent with the tendency of interviewees (training and HR managers) to report more often in quoted companies than in other organisations that they face an 'affordability' constraint from the finance function when making the 'business case' for apprenticeship training.

> '...the scope for pursuing social goals is likely to be greater in the public and the non-profit sectors than in the corporate sector.'

Nor is the issue restricted to the private sector. Some public sector and non-profit employers are subject to financial constraints not dissimilar to those in quoted companies. Even so, the scope for pursuing social goals is likely to be greater in the public and the non-profit sectors than in the corporate sector. The training practices of Leicester Council DSO in construction and BIGBORO council in IT Services reflect such objectives, as do those of the consumer Co-ops.

The potential relationship between ownership and community ties on the one side and training intensity on the other shows various exceptions even within the limited confines of our case studies. McNicholas and Tates are family firms, in construction and retailing respectively, that do not offer apprenticeships. Nor do Siemens Standard Drives and (for Level 3 Apprenticeships) BIGBORO, both of which have strong community ties.

Nevertheless, the case-study evidence, taken as a whole, suggests a moderate tendency for companies with concentrated ownership, and in particular family-owned ones, to operate a higher apprenticeship intensity than do other organisations, including co-operative and public sector bodies as well as 'stock market companies'. The statistical basis of these findings is presented in the Appendix.

Culture and tradition

The evidence also suggests a secondary role for sectoral tradition and regional culture as influences on apprenticeship intensity. The apprenticeship traditions of engineering appear to support above-average apprentice intensities in that sector. There is less agreement about the strength of these factors in construction, given the deleterious effects of the layered subcontracting that characterises the sector. Even there, the difference between the Scottish and English operations of Morrison suggests a role for tradition, in association with contractual practice. The company's apprentice intensity is much higher north of the border than in England, and, while subcontracting is less marked in its Scottish operation as well, the national tradition of respect for skill may play a part too.

CONCLUSIONS

The scale and intensity of participation among the case study employers who provide apprenticeship training is limited overall, and distinctly variable from employer to employer. Some programmes show low numbers or low intensity, including some operated by employers with established reputations for skills and training.

The limited number of apprentices that show up in most case studies – where they tend to be numbered in the dozens rather than the hundreds – reflect particular features of the modern business environment. The salient factors include, according to case and sector: the decentralisation of HR decisions to division and establishment level, and the associated loss of economies of scale in training provision; the outsourcing of non-core activities; and, in much of engineering and telecommunications, protracted employment reduction.

Of the many factors that potentially influence training intensity, the case studies suggest the importance of ownership structure and community ties. Organisations that are insulated from the pressures of the stock market by their ownership structures, particularly as unlisted family firms, and those that have deep roots in local communities, appear to opt for a higher intensity of training than do others who lack those attributes.

EMPLOYER PARTICIPATION IN ADVANCED APPRENTICESHIP: CONTENT

6

❖ **Collaboration between the employer and a Further Education college remains prominent in engineering and telecommunications, but no longer in construction**

❖ **In retailing, employer responsibility appears to have been extended by an 'employer does it all' approach, but this may be misleading**

❖ **Large employers often remain involved in the design and operation of apprenticeship even when they contract out not only the detailed work but also overall contractual responsibility**

The next issue is how those employers who participate in Advanced Apprenticeship actually do so. In particular, to what extent do they take responsibility for organising and delivering the training programme themselves, as opposed to contracting with external providers to do so?

The Cassells Committee urged that large employers increase their participation in what is now Advanced Apprenticeship not just by contributing on-the-job training and work experience to an Advanced Apprenticeship programme organised by an external provider, but also by acting as prime sponsors, taking responsibility themselves for the organisation and delivery of a training programme as a whole. The Committee recommended the development of a National Modern Apprenticeship Framework that would clarify the roles of the various parties, enhancing that of the employer, and downgrading that of the specialist provider to 'employer support agent' (MAAC, 2001).

APPRENTICESHIP RESPONSIBILITY

Table 9 (on page 32) shows that, of the eighteen cases that provide apprenticeships (both inside and outside Advanced Apprenticeship), nine are prime sponsors under Advanced Apprenticeship, that is, they themselves hold the contract with the LSC for the overall programme. (The sole non-AA employer is included in this category, despite not holding an LSC contract, as it organises its programme itself.) In the other nine cases, the responsibility is held either by a training subsidiary, a Training Board, or an independent provider. The pattern varies by sector. In engineering and telecommunications, the employer is prime sponsor in five cases out of six; in retailing, in three out of four. In construction, by contrast, only one employer (NG Bailey) acts as prime sponsor, though two others use a subsidiary to do so.

A related aspect of the employer's role is the extent to which particular components of the apprenticeship programme are contracted out to specialist organisations. In the post-war decades, Apprenticeship typically used to be organised around what might be called the 'traditional' approach: the employer organises and delivers the entire programme, except technical education, which a Further Education college provides part time, on day or block release.

> 'Apprenticeship...used to be organised around...the 'traditional' approach: the employer organises and delivers the entire programme, except technical education...'

That approach, elaborated nowadays to include explicit contractual relationships between the employer and the college, and often to include Key Skills as well as technical education, still dominates in some frameworks – as here in four of the six apprenticeship programmes in engineering and telecommunications.

In construction, only NG Bailey adopts the traditional approach. The other employers leave it to a training subsidiary, a Training Board or a specialist provider not only to hold the LSC contract but also to do most or all of the teaching and assessment required by the three programme components.

In retailing, by contrast, three of the four employers who provide apprenticeships perform all of the same teaching and assessment in-house. Two of them are customer co-operatives. The fourth, Lincolnshire Co-op, no longer takes on Advanced Apprentices. It has assigned all activities for those who remain in training to a part-owned specialist provider.

The congruence between these arrangements and the aspirations of the Cassells Committee is only moderate. A large minority of case-study employers do not sponsor apprentices. Of those that do, only nine act as prime sponsors in the occupations covered

Table 9   Content of apprenticeship provision (by case-study employers)

Frameworks[b]	No. providing apprenticeship	Employer selects apprentices itself	Prime sponsor (contract holder)				Provision of teaching and assessment[a]			
			Self	ITB[c]	Training subsidiary[d]	Independent provider(s)	All in-house	Traditional FE role[e]	Contract with private provider	Other
Engineering, telecommunication	6	6	5	0	0	1	0	4	1	1
Construction, engineering construction	7	7	1	3	2	1	0	1	1	5
Retailing	5	4	3	0	1	1	3	0	1	1
All	18	17	9	3	3	3	3	5	3	7

Note: includes the one provider of 'non-AA' apprenticeships (classed here as a prime sponsor), and one retailer who now offers Apprenticeship only in non-retailing occupations

a. Training and assessment of NVQ, Technical Certificate and Key Skills

b. No apprentices are taken on by any IT case-study employer

c. Industry Training Board (CITB or ECITB)

d. Includes joint ventures and partially owned independent providers

e. Subcontract to Further Education college for teaching and assessment of Technical Certificate (optionally, Key Skills too) but not NVQ here. Most of the other participants leave it to a Further Education college or training subsidiary to act as prime sponsor, but three of them use a commercial training provider.

All nine of the participating employers who do not act as prime sponsors insist that they remain closely involved in the design and operation of their Apprenticeship programme. One potential test of such statements is how apprentices are selected and the status they enjoy. Taking selection first, any willingness by an employer to leave that to an outside provider might be taken as evidence of low involvement. Smaller employers may be particularly prone to do that. In fact, all but one of the nine out-sourcing large employers select their Advanced Apprentices themselves, whether directly or through a training subsidiary. The one that does not select its Apprentices itself changed its practices after deciding to abandon the programme.

A second criterion is whether Apprentices enjoy employee status. The LSC recommends but does not require this, and any employer whose commitment to the programme is weak might want to refuse it, for the first phases of training at least. In fact, the 17 employers in question offer all participants on their Advanced Apprenticeships employee status from the outset. STEAMCO previously took on participants only after nine months of ECITB-sponsored training, but it now employs and pays them from the outset. BIGBORO's IT Services department does hold back employee status for a period the duration of which depends on Apprentice performance and its budgetary position, but it has not yet offered Apprenticeships at Level 3.

What the extensive use of external specialist providers means for employer commitment can be explored through four of the five cases that have taken that route (Box 9). All express a strong commitment to, and a sense of ownership of, 'their' apprenticeship programmes. All select and employ the Apprentices themselves, though the details vary from case to case. Two have in recent years moved back towards in-house provision.

BOX 9 LARGE EMPLOYERS' OUT-SOURCING OF APPRENTICESHIP

J.C. Bamford leaves all teaching and assessment of its Advanced Apprentices to two local Further Education colleges. The company selects the applicants itself. It left half of its Advanced Apprentice vacancies unfilled in 2004 rather than accept applicants whose personal qualities were judged defective.

BT contracts with Accenture, the management consultants, to provide all non-NVQ training and all assessment for Advanced Apprenticeships in field services engineering, as part of the wider out-sourcing of all of its HR functions. BT remains closely involved in the operation of the programme, and organises the on-the-job training around the country. The performance of the out-sourcing arrangement is subject to review, with the in-house alternative kept in view.

Leicester City Council's Maintenance DSO's apprenticeship programme has in the past used

---

commercial providers and Further Education colleges for training and assessment. Legal changes concerning gas safety have led the organisation to bring in-house all training, assessment and accreditation, except the Further Education component, thereby generating a considerable reduction in costs.

Siemens Traffic Controls previously used two external commercial providers in succession as prime sponsors of its (Modern) Apprenticeship programme for test engineers in manufacturing. Quality problems led it to cancel the programme. It has reverted to a traditional approach for its current non-AA apprenticeships for field services engineers, with external provision limited to ONC and HNC courses at Further Education colleges.

Not all employers are content to outsource significant parts of their apprenticeship programmes beyond the traditional Further Education component. NG Bailey in particular takes the view that relinquishing anything more than that would jeopardise its reputation for skills and training.

> '...the case studies...appear to negate, for large employers at least, the prospect that extensive outsourcing and complicated contractual chains cause not only administrative waste but also problems of control and accountability...'

Overall, however, the case studies therefore appear to negate, for large employers at least, the prospect that extensive outsourcing and complicated contractual chains cause not only administrative waste but also problems of control and accountability more generally. The same attributes can also bring benefits in terms of the specialisation of roles and economies of scale. Some large companies insist that outsourcing permits scarce managerial time to be devoted to higher value-added activities than compliance with the LSC's contractual requirements, which can be left to specialist, experienced providers.

The cases suggest then that, at least among large employers, both the extent and the disadvantages of outsourcing are limited, in that all participants show evidence of being committed to their training programmes. Any problems caused by contractual over-elaboration may be more common among smaller employers and more commercially oriented specialist training providers.

FINANCIAL CONTRIBUTION

One reason for wishing the employer to be more centrally involved in the organisation of Advanced Apprenticeships is an expectation that the committed employer will produce a better programme. In particular, the organisation may be expected to invest its own resources in the training, instead of limiting its outlay to the grants provided by the LSC, as specialist providers unavoidably must.

The extent to which employers actually invest resources over and above the LSC grant cannot be established in detail, given the difficulty of costing on-the-job training in particular. Nevertheless, some patterns can be detected in the case studies.

> '...the four engineering, construction, and telecommunications companies who provide estimates of their training costs...suggest outlays of between £40,000 and £65,000 per Advanced Apprentice.'

First, the four engineering, construction, and telecommunications companies who provide estimates of their training costs – which typically account for direct inputs only, are based on accounting rather than opportunity costs, and exclude public grants – suggest outlays of between £40,000 and £65,000 per Advanced Apprentice. Such costs dwarf the LSC maximum grant, estimated at nearly £15,000. In those cases, prime sponsorship is undoubtedly associated with a large investment by the employer in each apprentice.

At the other pole, the same does not appear to apply in retailing. The retailing employers who act as prime sponsors actually go one step further, in providing and assessing all components in-house. At the same time, they do not appear to invest significant amounts in their Advanced Apprentices over and above the public funds they receive. The LSC grant typically covers the costs of off-the-job training and all assessments. The employer is left to cover any costs incurred in on-the-job training in the event that the Apprentice is paid more than the value of his or her output. Since our interviewees typically stated that, in retailing, Advanced Apprentices become productive quickly, such costs are probably low, and possibly zero or negative in some cases. Other, more systematic evidence is consistent with such a picture (Hogarth and Hasluck, 2003).

> 'The wider educational merits of...Technical Certificates are...open to question...'

Finally, while the willingness of some retailers to provide all training and assessment themselves does suggest high commitment, their task is lightened by the low requirements of the sector's Technical Certificates. The 'guided learning hours' required in retailing are at most half those in construction and one-quarter those in engineering (see Appendix, Table A1). The retailing certificates can be 'delivered' by the employer's staff without external educational assistance. The wider educational merits of such Technical Certificates are therefore open to question, and with them the benefits of the employer responsibility for delivering the entire programme that characterises the sector.

Construction offers a more diverse but broadly similar picture. The employers who use a training subsidiary as prime sponsor typically expect it to finance itself, relying on public grants and revenues from training services sold to other employers. The employer itself then need inject no extra resources into Apprentice training – again, except insofar as Apprentices' pay exceeds their output value during on-the-job training. The Training Boards' programmes are, however, likely to require more of the employer than in the case of retailing – not only in terms of the payroll levy that funds the Boards' activities, but also because the Apprentices must spend more time studying for a Technical Certificate, and some of that time will normally be paid for by the employer.

The picture proves more complicated than any simple mapping of prime sponsorship onto a substantial investment in skills on the part of the employer. The two features are indeed positively associated in engineering, where prime sponsorship by employers is more the norm, and also in construction, where it has become rare. But they do not go together in convenience store retailing, which combines an extreme form of employer sponsorship (in-house provision of all components of the training framework) with an apparently limited employer investment in Apprentices' skills, over and above the public training grant.

CONCLUSIONS

The content of employer participation in apprenticeship is variable. The traditional approach, involving collaboration between the employer and a Further Education college, remains prominent in engineering and telecommunications. That is no longer the case in construction. In retailing, the scope of employer responsibility appears at first glance to have been extended by the 'employer does it all' approach favoured by some retailers. Their comprehensive approach to the employer's role is, however, potentially misleading, insofar as it reflects the limited training demands of the sector's training frameworks rather than a substantial investment of their own resources.

While half of the employers who provide apprenticeships outsource to external providers many of the activities involved, and even the overall responsibility for their programmes, it is not possible simply to equate prime sponsorship with commitment to apprenticeship, whether moral or financial. Large employers appear to remain involved in the design and operation of apprenticeship even when they contract out not only the detailed work but also overall contractual responsibility.

At the same time, the issue remains open. Some employers express reservations about the prospect of using, or the experience of having used, external specialist providers. This applies particularly when a commercially oriented body provides most or all programme-related services, as opposed to just a Further Education college providing mainstream technical education, or a group training association operating a training centre.

OPERATION AND DESIGN OF ADVANCED APPRENTICESHIP

7

❖ **The case studies suggest a trend towards an older and more qualified intake into apprenticeship, particularly in engineering and telecommunications**

❖ **Recent increases in the scope for educational progression through apprenticeship are limited**

❖ **The relatively low level of employer support for raising the educational contribution of apprenticeships is disappointing as the skill and developmental needs of these young people are not catered for in other ways**

We turn next to various attributes of apprenticeship that are relevant to its educational functions and its alignment with employers' HR practices. They are:

❖ the age at which apprentices enter training

❖ the qualifications required on entry

❖ completion rates

❖ educational content and progression

❖ the extent to which the public funding offered by the Advanced Apprenticeship programme induces employers to provide more or different apprenticeships than they would otherwise have done

❖ the tension in Advanced Apprenticeship between the goals of increased activity and an enhanced educational contribution.

The evidence again covers all training frameworks except IT, as our case studies include none of the few employers who offer Level 3 IT apprenticeships.

AGE OF ENTRY

Apprentices traditionally started on programmes at, or soon after, the last year of compulsory school attendance, which nowadays is 16–17 years of age. An incentive to maintain that pattern is still provided by the LSC's grants to employers for Advanced Apprentices, which fall for 19–24-year-old entrants to between one-half and three-quarters the rate for 16–18-year-olds, and – though this may change – to nothing for those aged 25 or above.

Employer practice varies considerably across the case studies. Seven employers – out of the seventeen who both take on

apprentices (both Advanced Apprentice and non-AA) and provided data – recruit two-thirds or more of their entrants at age 16–17. Two recruit at least half at age 18–20, and another two recruit roughly half at age 25 or older. Finally, two recruit similar proportions from the age groups 16–17, 18–20, and either 21–4 or 25 and above. The organisations with the largest shares of older apprentices are Leicester CC Maintenance DSO and Rolls-Royce, Derby.

> 'The six employers who recruit primarily among early school-leavers all come under the three traditional apprenticeship sectors...'

The factors that appear likely to cause such variation start with tradition. The six employers who recruit primarily among early school-leavers all come under the three traditional apprenticeship sectors: engineering, construction, and telecommunications.

A second factor may be the bias towards the youngest age category in the size of the LSC training grant, which encourages employers to focus on that age category. The influence of this factor might be expected to be stronger in retailing and parts of construction, where the LSC grant covers a large share of, or all, training costs, than in engineering, where it covers only a minority share. Public funding therefore fails to explain fully why interest in early school-leavers is greater in the traditional apprenticeship sectors than elsewhere.

A third influence is the supply of suitable applicants for training. It is often argued that, in an era of rising post-16 educational participation, Level 3–4 apprenticeship suffers increasingly from a scarcity of able and interested early school-leavers, and that employers therefore must turn to older and more qualified entrants in order to maintain their programmes.

The point is supported by both the several employers who have already done just that and evidence of greater recruitment problems among those who have not. In the latter category, J.C. Bamford, which recruits almost all of its apprentices at 16–17 years, has managed lately to fill only half of its apprentice vacancies. Mowlem South West, which recruits around 80% at that age, has encountered similar problems. By contrast, a large excess of qualified applicants over vacancies is reported by several employers who recruit more apprentices at age 18–24 than at 16–17, including BT and Rolls-Royce (Derby).

> '...the prospect of a career in convenience store management, with its lower pay and status, does not generate any surplus of acceptable applications over vacancies...'

Another factor is the appeal of the occupation and the employer as career prospects. Rolls-Royce and BT both offer the prospect of a well-paid career. By contrast, Bells Stores and Ipswich & Norwich Co-op, who also recruit many more 18–24- than 16–17-year-olds, find that the prospect of a career in convenience store management, with its lower pay and status, does not generate any surplus of acceptable applications over vacancies, despite their willingness to recruit after age 17.

APPRENTICE QUALIFICATIONS AT ENTRY

The engineering and telecommunications cases that train apprentices follow traditional practice, requiring applicants to have attained five 'good' GCSEs, by which is normally meant grades A–C in five subjects, including English and Mathematics. Most of them report an excess of qualified applicants, permitting them to recruit many young people whose educational attainments exceed requirements.

The same does not apply in construction, in which a number of the case studies accept applicants with far lower educational attainments. A number expect applicants to pass the CITB's entry test rather than to meet any GCSE-based requirement.

The retailing employers who provide Advanced Apprenticeships, who are predominantly convenience store operators, appear closer to engineering than to construction in this respect. One finds it cannot impose the 'five good GCSE' criterion, as it would like, but three others say they use that criterion or something similar (for instance, grade A–C in English and Mathematics only) and still attract enough qualified applicants to fill their vacancies.

COMPLETION RATES

In 2002–03, only 32% of Advanced Apprentices completed the entire training programme. Although completion rates have been rising, particularly if only the work-based component (NVQ3) is considered, they still amount to less than one in two, and eight points lower still if completion of the 'educational' components (Technical Certificate, Key Skills) is included in the criterion. The rates also vary greatly by area of learning. In the four considered

here, Table 3 (Chapter 1) shows that they ranged in 2002–03 from 46% in engineering to 20% in retailing.

> 'In 2002–03, only 32% of Advanced Apprentices completed the entire training programme.'

The reasons for low completion include the tendency of many Apprentices and employers to adopt a 'cafeteria' – that is, 'select only what suits you' – approach to the components of Advanced Apprentice programmes. There is also the limited learning content of some programmes (Winterbotham, Adams and Lorentzen-White, 2000).

Completion rates are expected to be above average when a large employer is committed to an apprenticeship programme. This is partly because the programme is likely to be better, to the extent that the employer itself invests in it, and partly because of a greater prospect of well-paid subsequent employment than in the case of programmes organised by specialist providers.

Fifteen case-study employers gave a broad estimate of their apprentices' completion rates. Only three report a rate of less than 80 per cent, and all cases in engineering and telecommunications lie above that line. The lowest rates are in retailing, where two convenience store retailers say that only one-third of Advanced Apprentices complete their programmes. The two construction employers whose Apprentices train mostly at Level 2 report rates of 15% and 60%.

> 'Non-completion is a sensitive issue and some interviewees' estimates may be too high.'

These patterns are similar to those in official statistics. Taken at face value, they suggest that most large employers see most of their Advanced Apprentices through to completion. The implications therefore appear favourable for educational progression, insofar as that is possible on the basis of the sector's recognised technical certificates. We are, however, reluctant to place much weight on our data on this topic. Non-completion is a sensitive issue and some interviewees' estimates may be too high.

EDUCATIONAL CONTENT AND PROGRESSION

The next issue is the extent to which the Apprenticeships programme supports educational progression, a potential source of appeal to young people and their parents. The importance of the issue does not arise from any expectation that most, nor even many, apprentices will progress to higher qualifications. Instead, the mere possibility of doing so can increase the appeal of apprenticeship by undermining perceptions of it as unavoidably a terminus rather than a way station (Steedman, Gospel and Ryan, 1998).

Support for educational progression is also a leading policy goal, as part of the construction of a 'vocational ladder' of educational attainment. The introduction into Apprenticeships in recent years of requirements for Key Skills and a Technical Certificate has reflected such aspirations. Concerning Key Skills, the Government's efforts to build progression into Apprenticeship frameworks are widely seen by employers as concentrating on the remedial (in the shape of the Key Skills requirement) and neglecting progression (in terms of promoting Level 4 Apprenticeships as well). Nonetheless, employers who rail against the former might still support the latter.

We asked interviewees whether their Advanced Apprenticeship programme provides participants with a 'realistic option' of progressing to higher education. Twelve out of seventeen respondents, including all seven in engineering and telecommunications, answer yes, the others no. Opinion in construction and retailing is evenly divided.

Several of the employers who state that educational progression is possible provide evidence in support of the claim. The most impressive is perhaps Rolls-Royce (Derby), around two-fifths of whose Advanced Apprentices now go on to a Higher National qualification (Certificate or Diploma) or a Foundation Degree before 30 years of age. BT Retail supports the most able 20% of its Advanced Apprentices to continue to study for another year after completion, whether for a HNC or as the first year of a higher education qualification.

The presence of a similar option appears less plausible in construction, given the low educational attainments of most entrants and the Level 2 qualifications at which most Apprenticeships terminate. The three construction employers who report favourable progression options all refer only to Apprentices who proceed to Level 3.

The situation in retailing again differs from that in the other sectors. The educational content of the sector's Technical Certificates is strictly limited. In one sense that helps employers and young people, as it means that even entrants with low educational attainments can complete an Advanced Apprenticeship. By the same token, the qualification provides an inadequate basis for educational progression – a move for which, as more than one employer insists, few prospective managers of convenience stores have the ability or the interest in the first place. Two retailing employers departed from this norm, in depicting Advanced Apprenticeship as making progression possible in their sector. Their optimism may be realistic, but only insofar as educational institutions set low entry requirements for vocational programmes, notably Foundation Degrees, in the retailing area.

> '...few employers support the idea of increasing the educational content of the programme...'

The other side of the educational contribution of apprenticeship is the extent to which it furthers the education of the majority of participants who do not go on to higher qualifications. The key issue here is the educational content of the training framework. On this issue, few employers support the idea of increasing the educational content of the programme, whether by increasing the

content of the Technical Certificate or by introducing part-time general education.

> 'One building employer stated that the existing Level 2 Technical Certificate is too difficult for most of its Apprentices.'

An increase in the content and level of Technical Certificates was favoured by only two respondents. One is a construction firm with a small apprenticeship programme. It finds that even apprentice-trained bricklayers could benefit from more technical learning. The other is a convenience store retailer, who finds that Apprentices need to learn more in the area of report writing and presentation. Other respondents were mostly opposed. One building employer stated that the existing Level 2 Technical Certificate is too difficult for most of its Apprentices.

Raising the general educational content of Advanced Apprenticeships is favoured by only three interviewees, all in engineering. Two point to their need as multinational companies for improved language skills in the workforce – though one feels that the teenage years are already too late to teach those skills cost-effectively, and the other would want the Government to fund such learning in full. The third welcomes the production of the more rounded individual that university education was said not to produce but apprenticeship can produce.

The general lack of employer interest in increased educational content in construction and retailing, the prior educational attainments of whose apprentices are lower, suggests little prospect of developing the educational contribution of apprenticeship there.

> '...educational progression is a serious prospect for significant numbers of Apprentices only in engineering and telecommunications...'

Our evidence suggests, therefore, that educational progression is a serious prospect for significant numbers of Apprentices only in engineering and telecommunications – and potentially in IT, were apprenticeship to take root there. Even there, employers' interest depends primarily on its relevance to their own needs. The evidence again indicates the extent to which, in large organisations, apprenticeship has been narrowed to overlap with HR policy. By the same token, the prospects for apprenticeship to form part of a vocational ladder of educational qualifications appear poor, outside engineering and telecommunications at least.

ENCOURAGING APPRENTICESHIPS VIA PUBLIC FUNDING

To what extent does the public funding offered by the Apprenticeship programme induce employers to provide more or different apprenticeships than they would otherwise have done?

The picture proves mixed. Slightly more employers judge themselves likely to respond to a withdrawal of public funding than would expect to remain unaffected by it. In terms of the size of their apprentice programmes, 10 employers – out of 17 who provide Advanced Apprenticeships and answered the relevant questions – say that their programmes would become smaller were the LSC grant removed. Engineering and telecommunications see equal responses in both categories. One large engineering firm would expect such a change to increase the sensitivity of apprentice numbers to downswings in the product market, but no more than that. Construction employers who would cut their programmes back outnumber those who would not by five to one, even though for some the LSC grant goes to the CITB rather than directly to themselves.

In terms of programme content, eleven respondents would remove or change components, while six would retain the training framework inherited from Advanced Apprenticeship. Those who would initiate changes include four employers who would remove Key Skills requirements, four who would remove or change the Technical Certificate, one who would drop NVQ assessment methods, and one who would customise its programme to its own requirements. The only apparent sectoral component is that three out of the four employers who would jettison the Technical Certificate are convenience store retailers, two of them co-operatives.

The other side of the coin is that a substantial minority of the case-study employers who participate in Advanced Apprenticeships depict their decisions concerning apprenticeship as unaffected in either size or content by the programme's subsidies and requirements. Moreover, of the majority that are affected, the changes involved would only be marginal, at least as far as content goes – notably the selective removal of Key Skills training, and the removal of Technical Certificates in retailing – where, ironically, they are the least demanding of all.

The pattern can be viewed from two perspectives. The first is economic, informed by an interest in 'deadweight'. The apparent insensitivity of several employers' decisions to the programme's existence raises questions about the value for public money that it achieves. That issue is set aside here, for two reasons. One is the limited quality of what is largely conjectural evidence. The other is the existence of countervailing criteria that might favour Advanced Apprenticeship even in the presence of high deadweight. Subsidies to employer training programmes constitute nowadays one of the few channels of industrial policy that the rules of the international trading system accept as legitimate.

The second perspective is the implication for employers' HR strategies. In the case of employers who say their apprenticeship programmes would not be affected by the removal of Advanced Apprenticeship, the implication is that those strategies are set by wider business considerations and nothing else. Indeed, the four engineering employers who fall into this category note that their apprenticeship programmes antedated Modern Apprenticeship and insist that the programmes function only because of wider business considerations. By contrast, HR practices in the other sectors, particularly in private employment, may be more open to influence by the Government.

FRAMEWORK REQUIREMENTS AND APPRENTICESHIP TARGETS

A prominent theme in the redesign of Advanced Apprenticeships is an increase in the acceptability of employers' bespoke training programmes and qualifications. The theme is particularly pronounced in the 'new' sectors, represented here by retailing and IT. In those areas of learning, Apprentice numbers have fallen recently, even with Level 2 programmes included.

All of the interviewees who indicated an active interest in such developments were employers in retailing or IT. In retailing, participants in Advanced Apprenticeships were joined by some non-participants, particularly department store chains, in calling for a greater adaptation of Technical Certificates to employer requirements.

In IT, where no interviewee participates in Advanced Apprenticeship, suggestions include recognising the bespoke vendor qualifications that have greater currency in the sector than do the NVQs and Technical Certificates recognised for Advanced Apprenticeship. One employer hopes to see recognition by the QCA, and consequently by Advanced Apprenticeship, of the Chartered Technician award of the Institute of Electrical Engineers (IEE). A similar change has already happened in retailing, lower down the skill ladder. Tesco's internal training programme for Level 2 skills has been accredited by the QCA and thereby become eligible for public funding under the (Foundation) Apprenticeship programme.

> '...one non-participant employer in IT services sees the current NVQ and Technical Certificates as insufficiently demanding...'

There is also the odd counter-current. One retailing employer strongly opposes the relaxations, both recent and proposed, of the sector's training requirements in pursuit of increased employer participation in the Apprenticeships programme. It would prefer to see more consistency of training requirements across sectors and a statutory basis for apprenticeship as a whole. Similarly, one non-participant employer in IT services sees the current NVQ and Technical Certificates as insufficiently demanding, and advocates instead the recognition of IEE qualifications for Advanced Apprenticeships.

> 'The probable price of any increase in employer participation will be a reduction in educational standards and in the scope for educational progression...'

These points lead us to question the extent to which the existing heterogeneity of framework requirements across frameworks and sectors should be allowed to increase in order to bolster employer participation in new sectors such as retailing and IT. The probable price of any increase in employer participation will be a reduction in educational standards and in the scope for educational progression – particularly in retailing, where both are already low.

CONCLUSIONS

The case studies suggest a significant, albeit uneven, trend towards an older and more qualified intake into apprenticeship, particularly in engineering and telecommunications. Some large employers actively support apprentices' progression to higher qualifications, including Foundation and first degrees. These changes suggest an improvement in the prospects for developing the educational contribution of apprenticeship, as has already occurred in several European countries.

The limits to such developments come with the increasing integration of Apprenticeship into employers' HR strategies. There is, first, the widespread lack of interest among large employers in extending the educational content of apprenticeship in general – particularly in construction and retailing, where the need is arguably the greatest. Second, large employers express interest in enhancing educational progression in apprenticeship only selectively, insofar as it dovetails with skill requirements and career advancement within the organisation.

Recent increases in the scope for educational progression through apprenticeship are indeed welcome. Their limited extent and the low level of employer support for raising the educational contribution of apprenticeship are, however, matters for regret, from an economic perspective as well as from a social and developmental one, insofar as the skill and developmental needs of young people are not catered for in other ways.

OPERATION AND DESIGN OF ADVANCED APPRENTICESHIP

CONACLUSION

This report has considered the relationship between large employers and apprenticeship. It draws primarily on face-to-face interviews with the learning and development-related managers of 30 large organisations, public and private, British and foreign-owned, in four training sectors: engineering, construction, retailing, and information and telecommunications technology.

We define 'apprenticeship' functionally, as a form of vocational preparation for intermediate skills, to which it was traditionally geared. It denotes here structured learning programmes that aim at certified occupational skills and contain a mix of work-based and off-the-job learning.

In relation to the Apprenticeships programme through which the Government currently supports apprenticeship, this definition restricts our study to what is now called Advanced Apprenticeship (AA), whose qualifications are pitched at Level 3. We also include apprentices who do not come under the Apprenticeships programme.

> 'In some respects...apprenticeship training is complementary to both recruitment and upgrade training.'

Four issues have been considered. The first is the extent to which employers use apprenticeship as a source of intermediate skills. Apprenticeship has both drawbacks and advantages for employers as a source of intermediate skills, as compared with two alternatives: the direct recruitment of skilled individuals and the upgrade training of less skilled employees. Each alternative can in particular circumstances be more cost-effective than apprenticeship. In some respects and in particular conditions, apprenticeship training is complementary to both recruitment and upgrade training.

Our case studies show considerable variety of practice, in terms of the relative importance of the three sources of skill. Not

surprisingly, recruitment tends to be preferred to apprenticeship when it is cheaper. Apprenticeship tends to be preferred to upgrade training when skills must be built on a substantial platform of technical knowledge and experience. Otherwise, upgrade training tends to be preferred, not only because of its lower cost, but also because of its superior adaptability to HR practices.

Apprenticeship occupies a significant role in some contexts partly because it too can offer advantages in HR terms – an attribute favoured by the 'employer-led' design of the Advanced Apprenticeship programme. The advantages that large employers frequently claim for apprenticeship include the socialisation of young people into the organisation's culture and the reduction of labour turnover. These benefits, which applied traditionally only to elite apprentices, indicate the extent to which apprenticeship has been reorganised in modern Britain. Its traditional links to occupational labour markets have weakened; those to the internal labour market operated by the large employer have strengthened. In several cases, these advantages of apprenticeship more than compensate the employer for a cost that is greater than that of upgrade training.

The second issue is the extent to which apprenticeship continues to function outside the Advanced Apprenticeship programme. We have identified and studied only a single case of an employer who opts to operate its apprenticeships outside Advanced Apprenticeship, but several cases of employers some of whose apprentices are not eligible for coverage by it, whether in principle or only in practice. The leading categories are graduate, adult, and technician apprentices. The importance of those categories, if nothing else, point to the importance for public policy of distinguishing between 'Apprenticeship' and 'apprenticeship' – ie, between the programme and the institution.

The limited role played by apprenticeship outside Advanced Apprenticeship nowadays does not, however, establish that apprenticeship would have died out without Government support. Its relevance to business needs ensures its presence in many organisations, several of which claim that the presence of Advanced Apprenticeship has little or no effect on the volume and content of their apprenticeship programmes.

> 'Concerns about low participation and limited commitment on the part of large employers have not abated...'

The third issue is the extent and manner of employer participation in Advanced Apprenticeship. Concerns about low participation and limited commitment on the part of large employers have not abated, despite the Government's efforts to induce more to participate. The pattern of participation in the case studies varies by framework and context. Many case-study employers participate, but a significant number do not. Some participants provide few places, but others provide many (relative to employment in intermediate skills). One in two case-study employers do not act as prime sponsors of their Advanced Apprenticeship programmes, but rather leave that task to specialist external providers.

> '...the most important consideration is the employer's response to training content proper.'

These patterns reflect, in addition to the factors that favour recruitment and upgrade training over apprenticeship, both the attributes of Advanced Apprenticeship itself and the specific attributes of the employer. Our evidence on the former suggests that the most important consideration is the employer's response to training content proper. Employers who value the relevant NVQ3 and Technical Certificate are more likely to participate than those who do not. By contrast, the other widely discussed attributes of Advanced Apprenticeship show little association with actual participation by case-study employers. These include both the attributes that employers generally welcome, including helping young people, access to public funds, and public relations, and those that they often criticise, notably administrative requirements.

Concerning the role of employer attributes, our evidence suggests that the intensity of participation is related to the ownership attributes of the company. Firms that are more insulated from financial markets, whether by unlisted status or concentrated ownership, appear to operate larger apprenticeship programmes – ie, to train more apprentices per skilled employee.

Our next set of issues concerns the educational aspects of apprenticeship, as reflected in: the age, prior qualifications, programme completion, and subsequent educational progression of apprentices; and employer attitudes towards both the educational enrichment of training frameworks and educational progression by apprentices. The practices of case-study employers are again highly variable. Some support a significant share of their apprentices to proceed to higher qualifications after completing their programmes. At the same time, few employers show interest in the educational enrichment of training curricula,

whether with additional technical or abstract knowledge, as a source either of increased learning by the average apprentice, or of expanding the minority of apprentices who opt for educational progression.

> 'The prospects for the Government's stated aspiration to develop Apprenticeship into part of a vocational education ladder remain bleak...'

The situation is particularly striking in retailing, where the educational demands of the relevant Technical Certificates are low, and some employers would like to see even that requirement scrapped. The prospects for the Government's stated aspiration to develop Apprenticeship into part of a vocational education ladder remain bleak in all sectors except engineering and telecommunications. Indeed, the abiding pressure to generate more Apprenticeship places threatens to make them bleaker: Sector Skills Councils increasingly accommodate employer-specific qualifications, in the hope of inducing more large employers to participate.

Our research suggests issues for employers in general, and HR managers in particular:

❖ In particular circumstances, employers benefit from the introduction or expansion of apprenticeship training. That is particularly likely when skilled staff are difficult to recruit, upgrade training cannot provide sufficient vocational knowledge, and apprenticeship increases employee loyalty and reduces labour turnover.

❖ HR managers need information about the relative costs and benefits of the different types of training conducted within the organisation, notably apprenticeship and upgrading, and how both compare with recruitment.

❖ Two particular potential benefits of apprenticeship deserve wider recognition: the scope for improving the selection and socialisation of young people who are prospective long-term employees, and for promoting linkages between educational progression and career advancement within the organisation.

❖ The extent to which the content of Advanced Apprenticeship can be matched to the individual employer's requirements should be more widely appreciated, particularly in the 'new' training sectors.

❖ In at least one case, the HR function appears to have only limited knowledge of the organisation's apprenticeship programme, in association with the assigning of responsibility for that kind of training to line management. In such cases, a greater integration of apprenticeship into the wider HR function appears desirable.

Some issues for public policy can also be indicated:

❖ *Employer participation.* Employers' willingness to participate in Advanced Apprenticeship depends primarily on how they perceive the technical content of the recognised vocational qualifications. Were the content of these qualifications altered in the direction desired by employers, the willingness of employers to participate would increase. In retailing, that would, however, mean a reduction in the already limited content of the Technical Certificate.

❖ *Vocational education.* The Government's wish to see Apprenticeship become part of a ladder of vocational qualifications has long been a reality in engineering and telecommunications. In construction and retailing, by contrast, its realisation would require the reform of training curricula – in particular, the injection of a more substantial component of technical education. Such changes cannot be expected from Sector Skills Councils at present, given the dominance of business interests in policy implementation and the Government's prioritisation of programme size over programme quality.

> '...the programmes of most large employers still attract an excess supply of suitable applicants.'

❖ *Appeal to young people.* Although the expansion of Higher Education has reduced the share of young people interested in apprenticeship, the programmes of most large employers still attract an excess supply of suitable applicants. Only in lower-paid sectors and occupations, including parts of retailing and construction, does the supply of potential apprentices to large employers' programmes warrant policy concern.

❖ *Apprenticeship activity.* It is desirable, given the needs both of individuals and the economy, for the apprenticeship programmes of some large companies to expand beyond the scale appropriate to their business requirements alone. How to engender that remains controversial, but one possibility is more cost-sharing for the more expensive skills. Some employers indicate a willingness to offer more apprenticeships were more of the cost to be borne by other parties – a category that potentially includes apprentices themselves, public bodies, and employer organisations.

❖ *Technician apprenticeship.* The limitation of LSC funding to Level 2–3 programmes has reduced the relative eligibility for public support of technician (Level 4) programmes. In sectors in which technician apprenticeship had already become established, including engineering, construction and telecommunications, the balance between its craft and technician components has been distorted. A rebalancing of public support between Level 3 and 4 programmes is desirable.

❖ *IT.* The scope for expanding apprenticeship is constrained with particular severity in IT (as in much of retailing) by employers' preference for graduate recruitment and upgrade training, and by high rates of labour mobility. It might be better to concentrate public effort on more promising terrain, and specifically to discourage Sector Skills Councils from diluting training standards in the quest for more apprenticeships.

❖ *Programme branding and coverage.* The Government has opted to apply the term 'Apprenticeship' to all DfES-funded programmes of work-based training for intermediate skills. That decision may have expanded training in some occupations. As, however, not all apprentice training has been made eligible for public funding, some employers validly criticise the decision as having caused confusion over the meaning of 'apprenticeship'. The Government might be asked to recognise the existence of non-AA apprenticeship, and to gauge its content, magnitude, and causes more systematically than has been possible in this project.

> 'The confidence that the Modern Apprenticeship Advisory Committee placed in employer-sponsored apprenticeship is broadly warranted.'

Finally, we note the variety of good training practice and the amount of innovation on view in the case studies, much of it including apprenticeship. The confidence that the Modern Apprenticeship Advisory Committee placed in employer-sponsored apprenticeship is broadly warranted. The need, as always, is dual: first, to induce the large employers who currently provide high-quality apprenticeships to expand their programmes; second, to raise programme quality in the sectors which are permitted, even encouraged, to aim low, in terms of skill level and educational content.

APPENDIX: FURTHER DETAILS OF CONTEXT, SCOPE, METHOD AND RESULTS

PUBLIC FUNDING

The amount of public funding available to organisations that act as prime training sponsors (ie hold the central contract with the LSC) varies with occupation, choice of Technical Certificate, and category of trainee. Table A1 on page 46 provides estimates based on various published components.

Public support for Level 3 training programmes in these four frameworks varies from £4,300 (19–24-year-old entrants to IT user programmes with the least costly Technical Certificate) to £14,800 (16-year-old entrants to engineering, IT services, or communications technologies with the most costly Technical Certificate).

TERRITORY

The primary focus is England. The limited attention paid here to the UK's other national entities reflects the decentralisation of training policies, which has seen the content of public programmes in Scotland, Wales, and Northern Ireland diverge from that in England. The Welsh Government does not require the external assessment of Key Skills in its Apprenticeships programme; the Scottish Government has not renamed its Level 2 programmes 'Apprenticeships'. Such differences lead us to concentrate on England, as the UK's largest national unit, but our cases include four employers whose headquarters or principal establishment is located in Scotland or Wales.

SOURCES OF EVIDENCE

We investigated these issues with case studies that involved face-to-face interviews with senior managers. Our evidence refers to the situation in the first half of 2005 (as the interviews were conducted between December 2004 and June 2005). We targeted large employers with significant numbers of employees in the occupations and sectors associated with each of the four

Advanced Apprenticeship frameworks, aiming initially at more than three case studies in each sector.

The case-study approach was chosen partly because of the limitations of statistical evidence in this field – a defect noted by the Modern Apprenticeship Advisory Committee and only partially remedied since (MAAC, 2001). A second reason was the importance of getting close to actual organisations in order to view apprenticeship in relation to HR practices. We asked interviewees to indicate a set of occupations that involved intermediate skills, into which apprenticeship does or could feed, for which data on employment, training, and recruitment could be provided.

We sought a set of employers that would both capture a variety of both contexts and skills-related practices, and suggest the determinants of those practices. Potential case studies were identified from prior knowledge, the trade press, external inspection reports, and the suggestions of knowledgeable individuals. Most of the organisations approached agreed to participate. Coverage was seriously affected by refusals only in IT, which has to date taken few Apprentices (Steedman, Wagner and Foreman, 2003). The only interviewees in ICT who provide apprenticeships operate in the telecommunications subsector.

Most of the 30 case-study organisations are listed companies. Of the eleven unlisted ones, four have a family controlling interest, four are co-operatives, and two are local authorities. We were not able to include central government, as intended, as the only potentially relevant framework is IT, and almost all IT functions are outsourced nowadays.

The interview-based evidence has been supplemented from telephone contacts with other employers, and from meetings with representatives of bodies with an interest in particular sectors' training methods, including the CIPD, Sector Skills Councils, employers' associations, and trade unions.

LARGE EMPLOYERS AND APPRENTICESHIP TRAINING

Table A1 ❖ LSC funding for completion of Advanced Apprenticeships by programme component and framework (authors' estimates), 2004–05

Age		NVQ3 National Rate (£)	Technical Certificate			Key Skills Amount (£)	Total (£)
			Guided learning hours	Amount (£)			
16–18	Engineering; IT Services, Communications Technologies	10,604	240–1,250	1,384–4,149		313	12,301–14,753
	Construction	9,789	450	2,163		313	12,265
	ITC; IT user	5,221	90–360	541–2,163		313	6,075–7,697
	Retailing	4,786	180–250	881–1,384		313	5,980–6,483
19–24	Engineering; IT Services, Communications Technologies	5,915	240–1,250	1,038–3,112		313	7,266–9,340
	Construction	4,691	450	1,622		313	6,626
	ITC; IT user	3,590	90–360	406–1,622		313	4,309–5,525
	Retailing	3,590	180–250	661–1,038		313	4,564–4,941

Sources: LSC, Funding: Indicative Rates for Further Education, Work-Based Learning and School Sixth Forms in 2004–05, Annex C; Funding Arrangements for Work-Based Learning for Young People in 2002–03, July 2002, pp64–5; LSC, Advanced Apprenticeship in Engineering, Framework Template, Framework Code 106, November 2004, Annex A; E-Skills UK, Apprenticeship and Advanced Apprenticeship for IT Users, Framework 322, p7; Apprenticeship Framework in Communications Technologies... Sector Code 232, p5; Apprenticeship Framework for IT Services and Development, Sector Code 292, p7; Skillsmart; and direct communication by CITB.

Notes: Guided learning hours are those specified for qualifications recognised as Advanced Apprenticeship Technical Certificates in 2004–05 are not available, the rates (by learning hours) for 2002–03 are used, increased by the inflation adjustments of 2.5% applied to LSC funding rates in each of the two subsequent years. Key Skills payments are based on published 2004–05 rates, on the assumption that no Apprentice undertakes more than the two required areas of learning. Estimates exclude additional payments by area (living costs) and personal disadvantage.

Information on case-study employers was collected through semi-structured interviews, using a detailed interview schedule. The schedule was piloted in the first three interviews and adjusted (marginally) in the light of that experience. Most interviews were conducted by two project members, on the organisation's premises, with one or more managers with responsibilities for training or HR/personnel matters. They lasted between 45 minutes and 3 hours, averaging around 75 minutes.

The case studies (Tables 4 and 5) are allocated by training framework according to the largest category of intermediate skills in their employment. The task is straightforward for all but two cases: Siemens Traffic Controls' apprenticeships for field services engineers are allocated to telecommunications rather than engineering; and STEAMCO's metalworking apprenticeships, to engineering rather than construction.

The stock of apprentices in case-study organisations is compared with the number of Advanced Apprentices active in the relevant

training framework in England in Table A2 below. The comparison, though far from exact, suggests that the coverage provided by our case studies is low in IT and engineering; moderate in construction, construction engineering, and telecommunications; but difficult to judge in retailing, given the inclusion of allied sectors in the official statistics.

RELATIONSHIP BETWEEN OWNERSHIP AND TRAINING INTENSITY

The statistical relationships between ownership attributes and training intensity across our case studies are shown in Table A3 on page 48. Most of the correlation coefficients are low, but the association of training intensity with family ownership is moderately large. In a small sample that was not selected at random, it is not possible to gauge the statistical significance of these correlations.

Table A2 ❖ Apprentice stocks in England by status and framework, late 2004

	1	2	3	4	5
	Advanced Apprentices[a]	Other Apprentices[a]	Both	Case-study organisation apprentices	
				Number	Share of framework[b]
Engineering	18,283	7,630	25,913	326	1.8
Construction engineering	633	239	872	120	19.0
Construction	3,868	10,986	14,854	2,761[c]	18.6[d]
Retailing	1,365	4,325	5,690	99	7.2
Telecommunications	2,747	452	3,199	471	17.1
IT	1,443	2,010	3,453	0	0
Sum (6 frameworks)	28,339	25,642	53,981	3,777	–
Sum (all frameworks)	104,002	108,091	212,093	–	–

Source: LSC, Quarterly Cumulative Starts and In Learning, August 2004 to January 2005, Coventry (http://lsc.fsite.com/cgi-bin/wms.pl/44)
Notes: a. Advanced Apprentices are on Level 3 programmes; other (Foundation) Apprentices, on Level 2 programmes
b. Column 4/column 1; includes apprentices not covered by Apprenticeship programme
c. Level 2 Apprentices included (Carillion and Laing O'Rourke cases)
d. Share of all Apprentices (column 3)

Table A3 ❖ Correlations between ownership attributes and intensity of apprenticeship training across case-study employers

	Ownership attribute[a]		Average intensity of apprenticeship[b]	Correlation with intensity of apprenticeship[c]
(1)	Listed company with dispersed ownership		5	-0.13
(2)	Unlisted company or listed company with concentrated ownership	All	12	0.25
(2a)	Unlisted company or listed company with concentrated ownership	Family-owned	16	0.32
(3)	Co-operative or public sector organisation		5	-0.05
(2)+(3)	All organisations except listed companies with dispersed ownership		8	0.18
	All		7	–

Notes: n=27

a. Binary (0, 1) variables in which the presence of the stated ownership attribute is coded '1' and its absence '0'. The two Japanese-owned companies are classed as listed companies with concentrated non-family ownership.

b. Number of apprentices (including non-AA ones) as a percentage of employment in the relevant intermediate skills occupations.

c. Simple correlation between ownership attribute and apprenticeship intensity across all cases.

REFERENCES

ALI (2004)

Annual Report of the Chief Inspector 2003/04. Coventry: Adult Learning Inspectorate.

ALMOND, P., EDWARDS, T., COLLING, T. et al (2005)

Unravelling home and host country effects: an investigation of the HR policies of an American multinational in four European countries. *Industrial Relations.* Vol. 44. 276–306.

APPRENTICESHIPS TASK FORCE (2005)

Final Report. London: Apprenticeships Task Force, DfES.

CIPD (2005)

Training and Development Survey 2005. London: CIPD.

DfES (2004)

Further Education and Work-Based Learning for Young People: Learner outcomes 2002/03. Statistical First Release SFR 04. 29 June. London: Department for Education and Skills

FERNER, A. (1997)

Country of origin effects and human resource management in multinational companies. *Human Resource Management Journal.* Vol. 7, No. 1. 19-37.

GOSPEL, H. (1994)

The survival of apprenticeship training: a British, American, Australian comparison. *British Journal of Industrial Relations.* Vol. 32, No. 4, December. 505–22.

GOSPEL, H. and DRUKER, J. (1998)

The survival of national bargaining in the electrical contracting industry: a deviant case? *British Journal of Industrial Relations.* Vol. 36, No, 2, June. 249–67.

GOSPEL, H. and FOREMAN, J. (2006)

The provision of training in Britain: case studies of inter-firm coordination. *British Journal of Industrial Relations.* Vol.44, No.2, June. 191–214.

GOSPEL, H. and FULLER, A. (1998)

The modern apprenticeship: new wine in old bottles? *Human Resource Management Journal.* Vol. 8, No. 1. 5–22.

GREEN, F. (2000)

The impact of training on labour mobility: individual and firm-level evidence from Britain. *British Journal of Industrial Relations.* Vol. 38, No. 2, June. 261–75.

GUEST, D., MICHIE, J., CONWAY, N. and SHEEHAN, M. (2003)

Human resource management and corporate performance in the UK. *British Journal of Industrial Relations.* Vol. 41, No. 2. June. 291–314.

HALL, P. A. and SOSKICE, D. (EDS) (2001)

Varieties of Capitalism. Oxford: OUP.

HOGARTH, T. and HASLUCK, C. (2003)

Net Costs of Modern Apprenticeship Training to Employers. London: Research Report 418, DfES.

KEEP, E. and MAYHEW, K. (1998)

The assessment: knowledge, skills and competitiveness. *Oxford Review of Economic Policy.* Vol. 15, No. 1. 1–15.

LEMAN, S. and WILLIAMS, P. (1995)

Apprentices and other long-term trainees – data from the LFS and other surveys. *Employment Gazette.* Vol. 103, No. 2. 67–74.

LIEPMANN, K. (1960)

Apprenticeship. London: Routledge and Kegan Paul.

MACDUFFIE, J.P. (1995)

Human resource bundles and manufacturing performance: organisational logic and flexible production systems in the world auto industry. *Industrial and Labour Relations Review.* Vol. 48, No. 2. 197–221.

MAAC (2001)

Modern Apprenticeships: The way to work. London: Report of the Modern Apprenticeship Advisory Commission, DfES.

MARSDEN, D.W. and RYAN, P. (1991)

Initial training, labour market structure and public policy: intermediate skills in British and German industry. In RYAN P. (ed.), *International Comparisons of Vocational Education and Training for Intermediate Skills,* London: Falmer Press.

OULTON, N. (1996)

Workforce skills and export competitiveness. In BOOTH, A. and SNOWER, D. (eds), *Acquiring Skills,* Cambridge: CUP.

PRAIS, S. J. (1995)

Productivity, Education and Training. Cambridge: CUP.

PURCELL, J., KINNIE, N. and HUTCHINSON, S. (2003)

Understanding the People and Performance Link: Unlocking the black box. Research report. London: CIPD.

RYAN, P. (1994)

Adult learning and work: finance, incentives and certification. In HIRSCH, D. and WAGNER, D. (eds), *What Makes Workers Learn: The role of incentives in adult education and training,* Hampton, Cresskill, New Jersey. pp11–36.

RYAN, P. (2000)

The institutional requirements of apprenticeship: evidence from smaller EU countries. *International Journal of Training and Development.* Vol. 4, No. 1, Janaury. 42–65.

RYAN, P. (2001)

The school-to-work transition: a cross-national perspective. *Journal of Economic Literature.* Vol. 39, No. 1. March. 34–92.

RYAN, P. (2004)

Apprentice strikes in the twentieth-century UK engineering and shipbuilding industries. *Historical Studies in Industrial Relations.* Vol. 18. Autumn. 1–63.

RYAN, P. (2005)

The institutional requirements of apprenticeship training in the context of the British Isles. In O'CONNOR, L. and MULLINS, T. (eds), *Apprenticeship as a Paradigm of Learning,* Cork: Cork Institute of Technology. pp15–34.

RYAN, P. and UNWIN, L. (2001)

Apprenticeship in the British 'training market'. *National Institute Economic Review.* Vol. 178, October. 99–114.

SKILLS TASK FORCE (2000)

Tackling the Adult Skills Gap: Upskilling adults and the role of workplace learning. London: Third Report, DEE.

SKILLSMART (2004)

A Skills and Qualifications Strategy for the Retail Industry. London: Skillsmart Retail Limited.

SPIELHOFER, T. and SIMS, D. (2004)

Modern apprenticeship in the retail sector: stresses, strains and support. Working Paper, National Foundation for Educational Research, London (http://www.nfer.ac.uk/publications/other-publications/downloadable-reports/pdf_docs/SKAJan04.pdf).

STEEDMAN, H., GOSPEL, H. and RYAN, P. (1998)

Apprenticeship: A strategy for growth. London: Centre for Economic Performance, LSE.

STEEDMAN, H., WAGNER, K. and FOREMAN, J. (2003)

ICT skills in the UK and Germany: how companies adapt and react. London: Discussion Paper 575, Centre for Economic Performance, LSE. (http://cep.lse.ac.uk/pubs/dp.asp?prog=CEPDP&pubyear=2003).

STEVENS, M. (1995)

Transferable training and poaching externalities. In BOOTH, A. and SNOWER, D. (eds), *Acquiring Skills,* Cambridge: Cambridge University Press.

TOMLINSON (2004)

14–19 Curriculum and Qualifications Reform, Final Report of the Working Group on 14-19 Reform. London: DfES.

UNWIN, L. and FULLER, A. (2004)

National Modern Apprenticeship Task Force Employers: Their perspectives on modern apprenticeships. Final report to Apprenticeships Task Force, Centre for Labour Market Studies, University of Leicester.

WACHTER, M. and WRIGHT, M. (1990)

Internal labour markets. In MITCHELL, D.J.B. and ZAIDI, M.A. (eds), *Economics of Human Resource Management,* Oxford: Blackwell.

WINTERBOTHAM, M., ADAMS, L. and LORENTZEN-WHITE, D. (2000)

Modern Apprenticeships: Exploring the reasons for non-completion in five sectors. London: Research Report RR 217, DEE.